JBoss EAP6 High Availability

Leverage the power of JBoss EAP6 to successfully
build high-availability clusters quickly and efficiently

Weinan Li

BIRMINGHAM - MUMBAI

JBoss EAP6 High Availability

First published: December 2013

Production Reference: 1171213

Published by Packt Publishing Ltd.
Livery Place
35 Livery Street
Birmingham B3 2PB, UK.

ISBN 978-1-78328-243-2

www.packtpub.com

Cover Image by Aniket Sawant (aniket_sawant_photography@hotmail.com)

Credits

Author
Weinan Li

Reviewers
Dustin Kut Moy Cheung
Jean-Frederic Clere
Ty Lim
Martin Večeřa

Acquisition Editors
Owen Roberts
Erol Staveley

Commissioning Editor
Sruthi Kutty

Technical Editors
Pooja Nair
Humera Shaikh
Ritika Singh
Nachiket Vartak

Copy Editors
Alisha Aranha
Roshni Banerjee
Sarang Chari
Karuna Narayanan
Deepa Nambiar
Kirti Pai

Project Coordinator
Ankita Goenka

Proofreader
Jonathan Todd

Indexer
Hemangini Bari

Graphics
Sheetal Aute
Ronak Dhruv
Valentina Dsilva

Production Coordinator
Shantanu Zagade

Cover Work
Shantanu Zagade

About the Author

Weinan Li started off as a Metro Railway Engineer and has worked at Alcatel since 2004 playing with hardware and assembly language.

He entered Red Hat in 2011 and is currently working as a Senior Software Engineer in the JBoss EAP team. He is also the productization leader of JBoss EWS and an active contributor to RESTEasy.

He currently lives in Beijing with his wife and their three-year-old son.

I would like to thank Veena Manjrekar from Packt Publishing who recommended me to write this book. I also give my gratitude to the editors from Packt Publishing, Sruthi Kutty and Ankita Goenka, who have given me great support during the writing process of this book.

I would like to thank my colleagues from Red Hat who have patiently answered my questions and helped me to review this book. They are Dustin Kut Moy Cheung, Fernando Nasser, Jean-Frederic Clere, Michal Babacek, Mladen Turk, Paul Ferraro, and Radoslav Husar. I would like to thank Martin Večeřa and Ty Lim who have given me a lot of advice.

I would like to especially thank Jean-Frederic Clere who has given me a lot of guidance during the writing process of this book. I would also like to thank all the people from the JBoss community who have inspired me to write this book.

Finally, thank you to my parents, my wife, and my son. I love you.

About the Reviewers

Dustin Kut Moy Cheung was born and raised in the island of Mauritius. Dustin's interest in computers was sparked when he obtained his first computer at the age of nine. Since then, he became determined to head into a career in the software world. He values spending time with his close friends, and looks at pictures of puppies and kittens in his spare time.

> I'd like to thank Weinan for giving me the opportunity to review this book. I'd also like to thank the awesome people at Red Hat, Toronto; you guys rock! To my friends scattered around the world, I miss you! And of course, I wouldn't be here without the unconditional love and dedication of my parents. Thank you Papi and Mami!

Jean-Frederic Clere was born in France, where he studied. After a few years of consulting work there, he started to write servers for applications and moved to Barcelona, Spain. In 2000, he started contributing to Apache Software Foundation projects. Since 2006 he has been working for Red Hat in the JBoss division where he takes care of the web layer and the Apache httpd as a proxy for the Application Server. Actually, he lives in Neuchatel, Switzerland.

> I would like to thank my wife Adelina for her patience with my geek behavior and all the colleagues and friends from Open Source communities who make my contributions possible.

Ty Lim is an experienced IT professional with more than 15 years' experience working on various operating system and middleware platforms. He has professional experience with IBM WebSphere Application Server, Apache Tomcat, Apache httpd server, and various other middleware and operating system platforms. He has experience working in various industries that include healthcare, telecommunications, financial, and software development. He holds a Bachelor of Science in Computer Science from the University of the Pacific, and a Master of Science degree in Computer Information Systems from Boston University.

I would like to thank my friends and family for their continued support.

To my "HH" friends, let's always keep the party going.

Martin Večeřa is a JBoss Quality Assurance Manager within a division of Red Hat. He has a passion for bleeding-edge projects and technologies. His main area of interest is Java middleware and performance testing in which he has almost 10 years' experience. Previously, he has developed information systems for power plants and medical companies. He publishes articles on Java middleware to various international and local web magazines and is a co-author of a blog on the PerfCake Performance Testing Framework.

www.PacktPub.com

Support files, eBooks, discount offers and more

You might want to visit www.PacktPub.com for support files and downloads related to your book.

Did you know that Packt offers eBook versions of every book published, with PDF and ePub files available? You can upgrade to the eBook version at www.PacktPub.com and as a print book customer, you are entitled to a discount on the eBook copy. Get in touch with us at service@packtpub.com for more details.

At www.PacktPub.com, you can also read a collection of free technical articles, sign up for a range of free newsletters and receive exclusive discounts and offers on Packt books and eBooks.

http://PacktLib.PacktPub.com

Do you need instant solutions to your IT questions? PacktLib is Packt's online digital book library. Here, you can access, read and search across Packt's entire library of books.

Why Subscribe?

- Fully searchable across every book published by Packt
- Copy and paste, print and bookmark content
- On demand and accessible via web browser

Free Access for Packt account holders

If you have an account with Packt at www.PacktPub.com, you can use this to access PacktLib today and view nine entirely free books. Simply use your login credentials for immediate access.

Table of Contents

Preface

High availability is a broad topic to discuss, and it concerns both project deployment and development. In this book, I'd like to explore the topics on clustering, load balancing, failover, and session replication.

High availability is also a very interesting topic, and the technologies provided by open source communities are especially fun. In this book we'll learn how to use JBoss EAP6 together with other JBoss and Apache community tools to build a high-availability system.

Here is a brief list of the projects we'll use in this book: JBoss EAP 6, Apache httpd, mod_jk, and mod_cluster. When I'm writing this book, JBoss EAP 6.1.0.Final is the newest product version based on JBoss AS 7.2.x and can be downloaded freely from the JBoss community. This version is very stable with its clustering features, so we'll use it in our book.

Since AS 8.x, the project name of JBoss AS has been renamed to WildFly. Though the project name changed, its design hasn't changed much, and you can reuse most of the knowledge in this book for future versions of WildFly.

JBoss EAP6 has provided a domain management feature that can help us to centralize the management of many servers. This feature is very helpful in a clustering environment, because we don't have to manage each server separately. We'll check this feature in the book.

Transportation security is usually considered critical in business applications. In this book, I'll introduce the methods of applying SSL into a clustering environment.

What this book covers

Chapter 1, JBoss EAP6 Overview, teaches you how to download and install JBoss EAP6, introduces you to startup modes of JBoss EAP6, and covers the basic uses of the domain management function.

Chapter 2, Using JBoss EAP6, covers more details on using the EAP6 management console and explains the design of the EAP6 management model.

Chapter 3, Setting Up a JBoss EAP6 Cluster, guides you on how to set the EAP6 servers properly for it to form a cluster.

Chapter 4, Load Balancing with mod_jk, shows how to use mod_jk as the load balancer of the EAP6 cluster.

Chapter 5, Load Balancing with mod_cluster, discusses how to use mod_cluster as the load balancer of the EAP6 cluster.

Chapter 6, Clustering with SSL, shows how to enable SSL in a clustering environment and teaches you how to set SSL to work with mod_jk.

Chapter 7, Configuring mod_cluster with SSL, shows how to set SSL to work with mod_cluster.

Chapter 8, Developing Distributed Applications, discusses how to develop the distributable applications with the help of JavaEE technologies and deploy it into the EAP6 cluster.

Appendix, WildFly Troubleshooting, shows how to debug the WildFly server at runtime. This chapter is available as a bonus chapter and can be downloaded from http://www.packtpub.com/sites/default/files/downloads/2432OS_Appendix.pdf.

What you need for this book

Some basic knowledge on Linux/Unix is required to read this book. You may need to follow the shell commands shown in the book to configure the servers properly.

Some basic understanding of IP multicasting is strongly recommended. Because many clustering features rely on IP multicasting, you can better understand the design of EAP6 clustering with this knowledge.

If you want to follow the instructions in *Chapter 8, Developing Distributed Applications*, you may need some basic knowledge of EJB and Servlet development. In addition, some knowledge on Maven usage is preferred.

Chapter 6, Clustering with SSL, and *Chapter 7, Configuring mod_cluster with SSL,* mainly focus on applying SSL in clustering. Some basic understanding of SSL/TLS technologies is needed if you want to follow the instructions in these two chapters.

When you are following the instructions in this book, please turn off the network firewall of your machine in case it blocks important ports needed by the cluster. If you are using Linux as your working environment, please disable SELinux because it will affect a lot on the clustering features. When you have fully understood the EAP6 clustering features, you can turn these protections back online and configure them properly to work with the EAP6 cluster.

Who this book is for

JBoss EAP6 administrators and JavaEE developers are the main audience of this book. Anyone who wants to know the coolest technologies provided by the JBoss community is recommended to read this book. I hope this book is not merely a step-by-step tutorial, so I've included some discussions on the design of JBoss EAP6 and relative projects.

Conventions

In this book, you will find a number of styles of text that distinguish between different kinds of information. Here are some examples of these styles, and an explanation of their meaning.

Code words in text, folder names, filenames, file extensions, pathnames, dummy URLs, and user input are shown as follows: "The default configuration file is `standalone.xml`."

A block of code is set as follows:

```
<interfaces>
  <interface name="management">
    <inet-address
      value="${jboss.bind.address.management:127.0.0.1}"/>
  </interface>
  <interface name="public">
    <inet-address value="${jboss.bind.address:127.0.0.1}"/>
  </interface>
</interfaces>
```

Any command-line input or output is written as follows:

```
$ ./standalone.sh
```

New terms and **important words** are shown in bold. Words that you see on the screen, in menus or dialog boxes for example, appear in the text like this: "To undeploy the project, click on **En/Disable** first and then click on **Remove**".

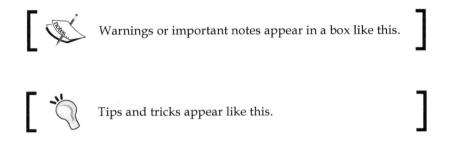

Warnings or important notes appear in a box like this.

Tips and tricks appear like this.

Reader feedback

Feedback from our readers is always welcome. Let us know what you think about this book—what you liked or may have disliked. Reader feedback is important for us to develop titles that you really get the most out of.

To send us general feedback, simply send an e-mail to feedback@packtpub.com, and mention the book title via the subject of your message.

If there is a topic that you have expertise in and you are interested in either writing or contributing to a book, see our author guide on www.packtpub.com/authors.

Customer support

Now that you are the proud owner of a Packt book, we have a number of things to help you to get the most from your purchase.

Downloading the example code

You can download the example code files for all Packt books you have purchased from your account at http://www.packtpub.com. If you purchased this book elsewhere, you can visit http://www.packtpub.com/support and register to have the files e-mailed directly to you.

Errata

Although we have taken every care to ensure the accuracy of our content, mistakes do happen. If you find a mistake in one of our books—maybe a mistake in the text or the code—we would be grateful if you would report this to us. By doing so, you can save other readers from frustration and help us improve subsequent versions of this book. If you find any errata, please report them by visiting http://www.packtpub.com/submit-errata, selecting your book, clicking on the **errata submission form** link, and entering the details of your errata. Once your errata are verified, your submission will be accepted and the errata will be uploaded on our website, or added to any list of existing errata, under the Errata section of that title. Any existing errata can be viewed by selecting your title from http://www.packtpub.com/support.

Piracy

Piracy of copyright material on the Internet is an ongoing problem across all media. At Packt, we take the protection of our copyright and licenses very seriously. If you come across any illegal copies of our works, in any form, on the Internet, please provide us with the location address or website name immediately so that we can pursue a remedy.

Please contact us at copyright@packtpub.com with a link to the suspected pirated material.

We appreciate your help in protecting our authors, and our ability to bring you valuable content.

Questions

You can contact us at questions@packtpub.com if you are having a problem with any aspect of the book, and we will do our best to address it.

1
JBoss EAP6 Overview

In this chapter, we will learn the basic concepts about high availability and have an overview of the functions that JBoss EAP6 provides to us in this field. Then we'll learn how to install JBoss EAP6 and see its basic usages.

Understanding high availability

To understand the term high availability, here is its definition from Wikipedia:

> *"High availability is a system design approach and associated service implementation that ensures that a prearranged level of operational performance will be met during a contractual measurement period. Users want their systems, for example, hospitals, production computers, and the electrical grid to be ready to serve them at all times. ... If a user cannot access the system, it is said to be unavailable."*

In the IT field, when we mention the words "high availability", we usually think of the uptime of the server, and technologies such as clustering and load balancing can be used to achieve this.

Clustering means to use multiple servers to form a group. From their perspective, users see the cluster as a single entity and access it as if it's just a single point. The following figure shows the structure of a cluster:

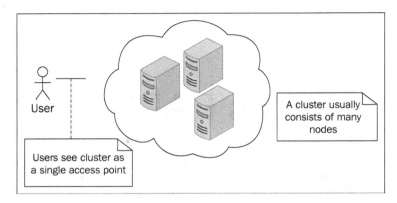

To achieve the previously mentioned goal, we usually use a controller of the cluster, called load balancer, to sit in front of the cluster. Its job is to receive and dispatch user requests to a node inside the cluster, and the node will do the real work of processing the user requests. After the node processes the user request, the response will be sent to the load balancer, and the load balancer will send it back to the users. The following figure shows the workflow:

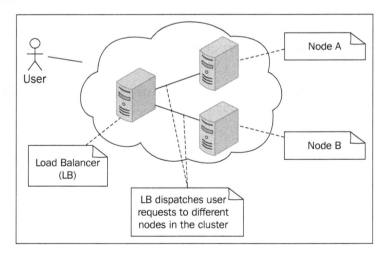

Besides load balancing user requests, the clustering system can also do failover inside itself.

 Failover means when a node has crashed, the load balancer can switch to other running nodes to process user requests.

In a cluster, some nodes may fail during runtime. If this happens, the requests to the failed nodes should be redirected to the healthy nodes. The process is shown in the following figure:

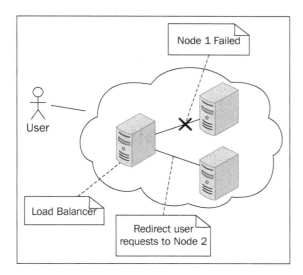

To make failover possible, the node in a cluster should be able to replicate user data from one to another.

 In JBoss EAP6, the Infinispan module, which is a data-grid solution provided by the JBoss community, does the web session replication.

If one node fails, the user request could be redirected to another node; however, the session with the user won't be lost. The following figure illustrates failover:

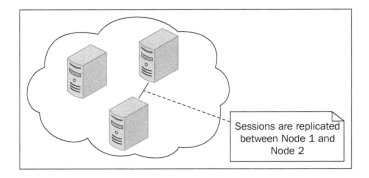

To achieve the previously mentioned goals, the JBoss community has provided us a powerful set of tools. In the next section we'll have an overview on it.

JBoss EAP6 high availability

As a Java EE application server, JBoss EAP6 uses modules coming from different open source projects:

- Web server (JBossWeb)
- EJB (JBoss EJB3)
- Web service (JBossWS/RESTEasy)
- Messaging (HornetQ)
- JPA and transaction management (Hibernate/Narayana)

As we can see, JBoss EAP6 uses many more open source projects, and each part may have its own consideration to achieve the goal of high availability. Now let's have a brief on these parts with respect to high availability:

JBoss Web, Apache httpd, mod_jk, and mod_cluster

The clustering for a web server may be the most popular topic and is well understood by the majority. There are a lot of good solutions in the market.

For JBoss EAP6, the solution it adopted is to use Apache `httpd` as the load balancer. `httpd` will dispatch the user requests to the EAP server. Red Hat has led two open source projects to work with `httpd`, which are called `mod_jk` and `mod_cluster`. In this book we'll learn how to use these two projects.

EJB session bean

JBoss EAP6 has provided the `@org.jboss.ejb3.annotation.Clustered` annotation that we can use on both the `@Stateless` and `@Stateful` session beans.

 The clustered annotation is JBoss EAP6/WildFly specific implementation.

When using `@Clustered` with `@Stateless`, the session bean can be load balanced; and when `@Clustered` is used with the `@Stateful` bean, the state of the bean will be replicated in the cluster.

JBossWS and RESTEasy

JBoss EAP6 provides two web service solutions out of the box. One is JBossWS and the other is RESTEasy. JBossWS is a web service framework that implements the JAX-WS specification. RESTEasy is an implementation of the JAX-RS specification to help you to build RESTFul web services.

HornetQ

HornetQ is a high-performance messaging system provided by the JBoss community. The messaging system is designed to be asynchronous and has its own consideration on load balancing and failover.

Hibernate and Narayana

In the database and transaction management field, high availability is a huge topic. For example, each database vendor may have their own solutions on load balancing the database queries. For example, PostgreSQL has some open source solutions, for example, Slony and pgpool, which can let us replicate the database from master to slave and which distributes the user queries to different database nodes in a cluster.

In the ORM layer, Hibernate also has projects such as **Hibernate Shards** that can deploy a database in a distributed way.

JGroups and JBoss Remoting

JGroups and JBoss Remoting are the cornerstone of JBoss EAP6 clustering features, which enable it to support high availability. JGroups is a reliable communication system based on IP multicasting.

 JGroups is not limited to multicast and can use TCP too.

JBoss Remoting is the underlying communication framework for multiple parts in JBoss EAP6.

Domain management

Besides the topics discussed previously, JBoss EAP6 has also introduced a new feature called **domain management**. This feature can help us to centralize the management of the EAP6 servers deployed as a cluster. In later chapters of this book we'll learn how to use this feature.

Installing JBoss EAP6

In the previous sections, we had an overview of high availability and what JBoss EAP6 provides to us in relation to this topic. It doesn't matter if you haven't understood all the things. We'll touch these parts in this book step by step to help you build the whole picture. The first step is to install JBoss EAP6. Please download `JBoss EAP 6.1.0.Final` from the following URL:

`http://www.jboss.org/jbossas/downloads/`

Locate the **6.1.0.Final** version and download the ZIP file. After the ZIP file has been downloaded, extract it. The contents are shown in the following screenshot:

```
● ○ ○                          3. bash
mini:jboss-eap-6.1 weinanli$ ls
JBossEULA.txt      bundles            modules
LICENSE.txt        certs              org
META-INF           docs               standalone
appclient          domain             version.txt
bin                jboss-modules.jar  welcome-content
mini:jboss-eap-6.1 weinanli$ []
```

From the previous screenshot, we can see a JAR file named `jboss-modules.jar`. This JAR file will help us to load the components of the server. The components of the EAP6 server are located in the `modules` directory. This directory contains the components of EAP6 that could be loaded by `jboss-modules.jar`.

The `bin` directory contains the start script and other tools that we'll use later.

The `standalone` and `domain` directories are related with the EAP6 startup mode. We'll cover it in more detail in the next section.

The JBoss EAP6 startup mode

The startup mode is a new concept introduced in JBoss EAP6. There are currently two modes provided by EAP6:

- The standalone mode
- The domain mode

And there are two startup scripts in the `bin` directory for these two modes:

```
domain.sh      standalone.sh
```

Let's see the meanings of these two modes.

The domain mode

The domain mode is a new concept introduced in EAP6. A domain means a group of servers that can share configuration/deployment information, which is very useful in a clustering environment.

For example, we have the three JBoss EAP6 servers running, and they form a cluster. Suppose we have a project called `cluster-demo` and want to deploy it to the cluster. The traditional method is to deploy this project to each EAP6 instance manually.

Fortunately, with the help of the domain management function in EAP6, we can now configure many EAP6 servers as a server group and deploy a project into this group. Then the project will be deployed into all the EAP6 servers that belong to this group. The domain mode provides a centralized management point to our cluster. The server group also shares the same configuration that is automatically distributed to all nodes. We'll see its usage in later chapters.

The standalone mode

The standalone mode is like the traditional JBoss AS running mode, and it doesn't have any domain management features supported during runtime.

Starting JBoss EAP6 in the standalone mode

Let's now try to start JBoss EAP6 in the standalone mode. Go to the `bin` directory and run `standalone.sh`. The server output is shown in the following screenshot:

```
● ○ ○                          3. bash
mini:bin weinanli$ ./standalone.sh
==========================================================================
====

  JBoss Bootstrap Environment

  JBOSS_HOME: /packt/jboss-eap-6.1

  JAVA: java

  JAVA_OPTS:  -server -XX:+UseCompressedOops -Xms1303m -Xmx1303m -XX:
MaxPermSize=256m -Djava.net.preferIPv4Stack=true -Djboss.modules.syst
em.pkgs=org.jboss.byteman -Djava.awt.headless=true


==========================================================================
====

23:34:31,693 INFO  [org.jboss.modules] (main) JBoss Modules version 1
.2.0.Final-redhat-1
23:34:32,340 INFO  [org.jboss.msc] (main) JBoss MSC version 1.0.4.GA-
redhat-1
23:34:32,420 INFO  [org.jboss.as] (MSC service thread 1-6) JBAS015899
: JBoss EAP 6.1.0.GA (AS 7.2.0.Final-redhat-8) starting
```

Now let's look at some details on the server output to understand the startup process.

Understanding the startup process

We can see several important things from the server output. The following is the first one:

```
Started 123 of 177 services (53 services are passive or on-demand)
```

From the previous log, we can see that not all the components are started during the EAP6 startup process. This design greatly speeds up the startup time of EAP6. We can see that some services are started by default during the start process:

```
19:50:40,812 INFO  [org.jboss.as.clustering.infinispan] (ServerServic
e Thread Pool -- 31) JBAS010280: Activating Infinispan subsystem.
19:50:40,815 INFO  [org.jboss.as.security] (ServerService Thread Pool
 -- 44) JBAS013101: Activating Security Subsystem
19:50:40,819 INFO  [org.jboss.as.osgi] (ServerService Thread Pool --
39) JBAS011906: Activating OSGi Subsystem
19:50:40,821 INFO  [org.jboss.as.naming] (ServerService Thread Pool -
- 38) JBAS011800: Activating Naming Subsystem
19:50:40,826 INFO  [org.jboss.as.security] (MSC service thread 1-12)
JBAS013100: Current PicketBox version=4.0.9.Final-redhat-1
19:50:40,846 INFO  [org.jboss.as.webservices] (ServerService Thread P
ool -- 48) JBAS015537: Activating WebServices Extension
19:50:40,859 INFO  [org.jboss.as.connector.logging] (MSC service thre
ad 1-6) JBAS010408: Starting JCA Subsystem (JBoss IronJacamar 1.0.11.
Final-redhat-1)
19:50:40,894 INFO  [org.jboss.as.naming] (MSC service thread 1-16) JB
AS011802: Starting Naming Service
19:50:40,903 INFO  [org.jboss.as.mail.extension] (MSC service thread
```

These components are called subsystems. These subsystems are configured in the standalone.xml file upon navigating through standalone/configuration.

Now let's see the actual command in standalone.sh that starts the EAP6 server:

```
eval \"$JAVA\" -D\"[Standalone]\" $JAVA_OPTS \
    \"-Dorg.jboss.boot.log.file=$JBOSS_LOG_DIR/server.log\" \
    \"-Dlogging.configuration=file:$JBOSS_CONFIG_DIR/
      logging.properties\"    \
    -jar \"$JBOSS_HOME/jboss-modules.jar\" \
    -mp \"${JBOSS_MODULEPATH}\" \
    -jaxpmodule "javax.xml.jaxp-provider" \
org.jboss.as.standalone \
    -Djboss.home.dir=\"$JBOSS_HOME\" \
-Djboss.server.base.dir=\"$JBOSS_BASE_DIR\" \
    "$SERVER_OPTS" "&"
```

Downloading the example code

You can download the example code files for all Packt Publishing books you have purchased from your account at http://www.packtpub.com. If you purchased this book elsewhere, you can visit http://www.packtpub.com/support and register to have the files e-mailed directly to you.

From the previous command, we can see that jboss-modules.jar is the bootstrap JAR file for the whole EAP6 server, and the entry point is org.jboss.as.standalone, which is specified in the following command:

```
-jar \"$JBOSS_HOME/jboss-modules.jar\" org.jboss.as.standalone
```

We'll see more details about the startup process later. Now let's check the configuration file of the standalone mode.

The standalone.xml file

The structure of standalone.xml is as follows:

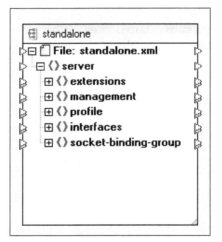

As shown in the previous screenshot, **standalone.xml** defines multiple aspects of the standalone service. Let's have a brief view:

extensions	This section contains a list of extension modules. The components listed here will be loaded by `jboss-modules`.
management	This section contains the configuration related to management interfaces of EAP6 and its security settings.
profile	In this section, we can configure the settings for each subsystem. Most of the subsystems are the components loaded in the extensions section, and some subsystems are required by EAP6 internally and loaded at startup by default.
interfaces	This section defines a list of named network interfaces.
socket-binding group	This section contains a list of socket-binding groups, including the set of interfaces that could be used by different modules.

Alternative configuration files

Besides the default file `standalone.xml`, EAP6 has provided some other profiles for the standalone mode.

 There is only one profile per standalone configuration file. In contrast, multiple profiles could be defined in the domain configuration file.

We can check them in the `standalone/configuration` directory:

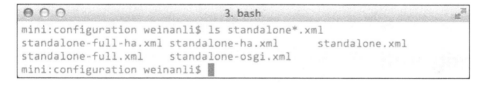

```
mini:configuration weinanli$ ls standalone*.xml
standalone-full-ha.xml standalone-ha.xml        standalone.xml
standalone-full.xml     standalone-osgi.xml
mini:configuration weinanli$
```

These files define the different profiles for different purposes. The following is a summary of their differences:

standalone.xml	This is the default setting of standalone mode.
standalone-full. xml	Compared with the default settings, this profile has added the messaging subsystem (HornetQ and relative components).
standalone-ha. xml	Compared with the default settings, this profile has added clustering-related components: mod_cluster and JGroups, replicable caches powered by Infinispan, and other relative components.
standalone-full-ha.xml	Compared with the default setting, this profile provides a combination of functions in '-full' and '-ha'.

To use these alternative configurations during startup, we can use the -c option when calling standalone.sh. For example, if we want to use standalone-ha.xml, the command is as follows:

```
$ ./standalone.sh -c standalone-ha.xml
```

Please note that the -c option assumes that the configuration is located at $JBOSS_HOME/standalone/.

The --help option

Both standalone.sh and domain.sh provide us with the help document. We can always use the --help option to check it:

```
$ standalone.sh --help
```

Configuration files

In the bin directory, there are several configuration files that will be included during the startup process:

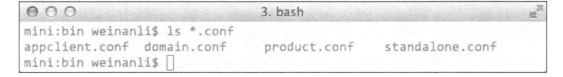

```
mini:bin weinanli$ ls *.conf
appclient.conf   domain.conf      product.conf     standalone.conf
mini:bin weinanli$ ▯
```

We can put our own configuration into these files, and it will be included by the startup scripts.

Starting JBoss EAP6 in the domain mode

In this section, let's have a look at the domain mode. Use the following command in the `bin` directory to start the EAP6 server in the domain mode:

```
$ ./domain.sh
```

We can see that the startup process is different with the standalone mode. Firstly, there are many more components loaded in the domain mode:

```
Started 274 of 401 services (126 services are passive or on-demand)
```

And in `domain.sh`, we can see that the startup command is also different:

```
eval \"$JAVA\" -D\"[Process Controller]\"
  $PROCESS_CONTROLLER_JAVA_OPTS \
      \"-Dorg.jboss.boot.log.file=$JBOSS_LOG_DIR/process-
        controller.log\" \
      \"-Dlogging.configuration=file:$JBOSS_CONFIG_DIR/
        logging.properties\"   \
      -jar \"$JBOSS_HOME/jboss-modules.jar\" \
      -mp \"${JBOSS_MODULEPATH}\" \
org.jboss.as.process-controller \
      -jboss-home \"$JBOSS_HOME\" \
      -jvm \"$JAVA_FROM_JVM\" \
      -mp \"${JBOSS_MODULEPATH}\" \
      -- \
      \"-Dorg.jboss.boot.log.file=$JBOSS_LOG_DIR/host-
        controller.log\" \
      \"-Dlogging.configuration=file:$JBOSS_CONFIG_DIR/
        logging.properties\"   \
      $HOST_CONTROLLER_JAVA_OPTS \
      -- \
      -default-jvm \"$JAVA_FROM_JVM\" \
      '"$@"'
'jboss-modules.jar' is still used for bootstrap:
-jar \"$JBOSS_HOME/jboss-modules.jar\" \
```

Compared with the standalone mode, the entry point is no longer `org.jboss.as.standalone`; instead, it becomes `process-contoller`:

```
org.jboss.as.process-controller
```

There is also a process called `host-controller`:

```
-Dorg.jboss.boot.log.file=$JBOSS_LOG_DIR/host-controller.log
```

The following figure shows the relationship of these processes when EAP6 is running in the domain mode:

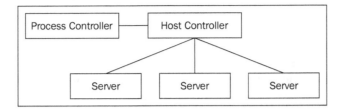

As in the domain mode, a lightweight **Process Controller** is started first, and then it spawns a **Host Controller** process that will control multiple server processes. This is because in the domain mode it allows multiple server instances to run at the same time, and each server will have its own JVM process.

The domain mode

As we have seen previously, when EAP6 is running in the domain mode, multiple severs can run at the same time. In addition, these servers can belong to different server groups. The servers that belong to the same group will share the deployment and configuration information.

For example, we have a server group called the **main-server-group**, and in this group, we have two servers called **server-one** and **server-two**. If we deploy a project called `cluster-demo.war` in the **main-server-group**, then it will be deployed into both the servers at the same time. And if we change some settings in this group, the settings of these two servers will all get synced:

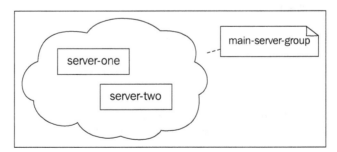

In the previous example the two servers of the same group are in the same machine and the same EAP6 instance. But actually they can exist in different EAP6 servers, and the servers in the same group can be synced across the network.

Configuration files

Unlike the standalone mode, the domain mode uses two configuration files:

- `domain.xml`
- `host.xml`

These configuration files are in the location `domain/configuration/`. Now let's have a look at `domain.xml` first.

The domain.xml file

The structure of the `domain.xml` file and its difference with `standalone.xml` are shown in the following screenshot:

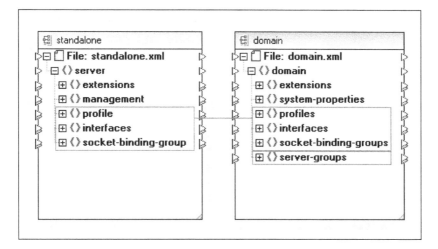

If we compare its structure with the standalone mode, we can see the differences. Firstly there are three sections in plural form:

- **profiles**
- **interfaces**
- **socket-binding-groups**

The reason for this difference is easy to guess. In the domain mode, there are multiple servers running in different server groups, and EAP6 supports each server group to have its own set of settings. So, different profiles, interfaces, and socket-binding-groups will be needed.

In addition, we can see a new section called **server-groups**. Here is its default setting in domain.xml:

```
<server-groups>
  <server-group name="main-server-group" profile="full">
  <socket-binding-group ref="full-sockets"/>
</server-group>
<server-group name="other-server-group" profile="full-ha">
  <socket-binding-group ref="full-ha-sockets"/>
  </server-group>
</server-groups>
```

The previous settings are shown in the following figure:

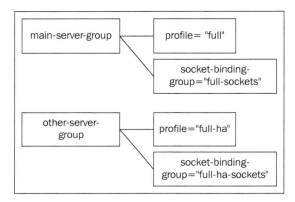

In this way, different server groups are bound to different settings.

The host.xml file

Now let's check host.xml. The following screenshot shows its structure:

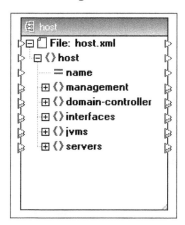

The `host.xml` file is the setting file for the host controller. It has some parts similar to `standalone.xml` such as management and interfaces. Their purposes are also the same. Now let's see the **domain-controller** section.

The domain-controller section

The **domain-controller** section defines which host is used as the domain controller. The domain controller is actually a host controller, but it acts as the manager of the domain. The default **domain-controller** is set to `local`, which means EAP6 will use its host controller as its domain controller by default.

We can also define a remote host controller as the domain controller. Then multiple EAP6 could connect to the same domain controller and accept its management. Now let's see the **servers** section.

The servers section

The **servers** section is shown in the following screenshot:

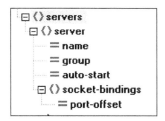

In the domain mode, a host controller can manage several servers at the same time, and each server has their own name and belongs to a server group; these servers are bound to different sockets to avoid conflicts.

The **auto-start** option checks whether to start this server during the EAP6 startup. We may choose which server to start during the EAP6 startup by this option.

The **port-offset** option is used to bind different servers into different ports to avoid conflict. Let's see the default configuration in `host.xml`:

```
<servers>
  <server name="server-one" group="main-server-group">
    <socket-bindings port-offset="0"/>
  </server>
  <server name="server-two" group="main-server-group">
    <socket-bindings port-offset="150"/>
  </server>
```

```
        <server name="server-three" group="other-server-group">
          <socket-bindings port-offset="250"/>
        </server>
</servers>
```

The following is the deployment diagram that shows the relationship between the previously discussed servers and server groups:

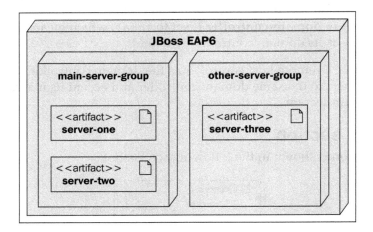

Here are the server group settings in `domain.xml`:

```
<server-groups>
  <server-group name="main-server-group" profile="full">
    <socket-binding-group ref="full-sockets"/>
  </server-group>
  <server-group name="other-server-group" profile="full-ha">
    <socket-binding-group ref="full-ha-sockets"/>
  </server-group>
</server-groups>
```

We can see that the **main-server-group** is bound to `full-sockets`, and the **other-server-group** is bound to `full-ha-sockets`. These two sockets are defined as follows:

```
<socket-binding-group name="full-sockets" default-
    interface="public">
  <socket-binding name="http" port="8080"/>
</socket-binding-group>
<socket-binding-group name="full-ha-sockets" default-
    interface="public">
  <socket-binding name="http" port="8080"/>
</socket-binding-group>
```

The `full-sockets` binds to the HTTP port 8080, and `port-offset` is 0. So the web port used by **server-one** is 8080; for **server-two**, because its `port-offset` is 150, its web port is 8080 + 150 = 8230. Similarly, the HTTP port used by **server-three** is 8080 + 250 = 8330.

Now let's set **auto-start** for all three servers to `true` so that they will be started during the EAP6 startup:

```
<servers>
  <server name="server-one" group="main-server-group" auto-
    start="true">...</server>
  <server name="server-two" group="main-server-group" auto-
    start="true">...</server>
  <server name="server-three-master" group="other-server-group"
    auto-start="true">...</server>
</servers>
```

Now let's start EAP6 in the domain mode by calling `domain.sh`. After EAP6 starts, let's try to access 8080, 8230, and 8330 with `telnet` commands:

```
$ telnet localhost 8080
Trying localhost...
Connected to localhost.

$ telnet localhost 8230
Trying localhost...
Connected to localhost.

$ telnet localhost 8330
Trying localhost...
Connected to localhost.
```

We can see all the servers are listening for connections now.

XSD documents

JBoss EAP6 has provided the schema documents in `docs/schema`. Each schema has defined a namespace used by the EAP6 configuration file. For example, we can check the beginning of `standalone.xml` and see the xml namespace it's using:

```
<?xml version='1.0' encoding='UTF-8'?>
<server xmlns="urn:jboss:domain:1.4">
...
```

We can see that the namespace used is `urn:jboss:domain:1.4`. Let's find the defined namespace in the `docs/schema` directory by using the `grep` command:

```
$ grep -rl 'urn:jboss:domain:1.4' *

jboss-as-config_1_4.xsd
```

We can see that `jboss-as-config_1_4.xsd` contains the definition of the xml namespace we are searching for. Now we can check the definitions for each element in this namespace. For example, if we want to understand the meaning of the **server** section in `standalone.xml`, we can check its definition in the `xsd` file:

```
<xs:element name="server">
  <xs:annotation>
  <xs:documentation>
    Root element for a document specifying the configuration
    of a single "standalone" server that does not operate
    as part of a domain...
  </xs:documentation>
  </xs:annotation>
    ...
</xs:element>
```

As we have seen in the previous code snippet, the `xsd` schemas are very useful documents. They can help us to understand the meaning of the elements in configuration files.

Summary

In this chapter, we have learned the basic concepts of high availability, and we have learned how to install JBoss EAP6 and run it in different modes. We also learned about the two running modes of EAP6. In the next chapter, we will learn to use the EAP6 management console, and we'll use it to deploy projects into EAP6.

2
Using JBoss EAP6

In the previous chapter, we have learned how to download and install JBoss EAP6. We also looked at the standalone mode and the domain mode of EAP6; in this chapter we'll start learning its basic usages. We will learn how to manage and configure the EAP6 server. The following topics will be covered in this chapter:

- Using the JBoss EAP6 management console to deploy a web application
- Basic usages of the Command Line Interface management console
- The design of the JBoss EAP6 management model

First, we need to understand some basic configurations of the EAP6 management console. After configuring it properly, we can start the EAP6 server and use its management console.

Configuring the JBoss EAP6 management console

JBoss EAP6 has provided two management consoles — one is based on the web and another based on the **Command Line Interface (CLI)**.Before using them, we need to configure the management modules properly.

Security realms

To use the management console, we must understand its authentication scheme. The authentication module used by JBoss EAP6 is called **security realms**.

> EAP6 uses security realms to gain secure access to the management interfaces.

Open `standalone.xml` in the standalone configuration. The relative settings are given as follows:

```
<management>
  <security-realms>
    <security-realm name="ManagementRealm">
      <authentication>
        <local default-user="$local"/>
        <properties path="mgmt-users.properties" relative-
          to="jboss.server.config.dir"/>
      </authentication>
    </security-realm>
  </security-realms>
  <management-interfaces>
    <native-interface security-realm="ManagementRealm">
      <socket-binding native="management-native"/>
    </native-interface>
    <http-interface security-realm="ManagementRealm">
      <socket-binding http="management-http"/>
    </http-interface>
  </management-interfaces>
</management>
```

As shown in the preceding configuration, the realm that is used by the management module is called `ManagementRealm`. It's using a property file called `mgmt-users.properties` to store the user's password information. The `management-interfaces` defines the network socket that is bound to the management console. By default, the web management console is bound to the address `127.0.0.1:9990`, and the CLI is bound to the address `127.0.0.1:9999`. The following diagram gives a summary of the management console configuration:

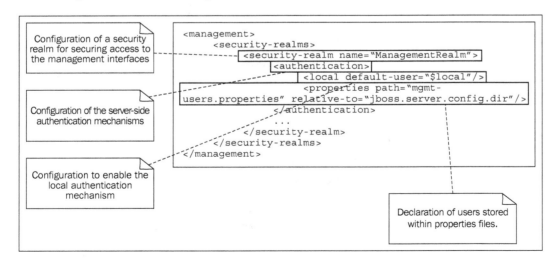

Since we have understood the authentication scheme used by JBoss EAP6, we now need to create a user account to access the management console.

Setting up an admin account

JBoss EAP6 has provided a command-line tool to generate user accounts for us. You will find it with the name `add-user.sh` in the `bin` folder. Let's use it to generate an administrator account. This process is shown in the following screenshot:

```
⊖ ○ ○                          2. bash
mini:bin weinanli$ ./add-user.sh

What type of user do you wish to add?
 a) Management User (mgmt-users.properties)
 b) Application User (application-users.properties)
(a): a

Enter the details of the new user to add.
Realm (ManagementRealm) :
Username : jbossadmin
Password :
Re-enter Password :
About to add user 'jbossadmin' for realm 'ManagementRealm'
Is this correct yes/no? yes
Added user 'jbossadmin' to file '/packt/jboss-eap-6.1/standalone/conf
iguration/mgmt-users.properties'
Added user 'jbossadmin' to file '/packt/jboss-eap-6.1/domain/configur
ation/mgmt-users.properties'
Is this new user going to be used for one AS process to connect to an
other AS process?
e.g. for a slave host controller connecting to the master or for a Re
moting connection for server to server EJB calls.
yes/no? no
mini:bin weinanli$ ▯
```

In the process shown in the preceding screenshot, we create a user named `jbossadmin` of the type **Management User**. This user belongs to the `ManagementRealm`, so we can use it to access the management console. Please note that the password must be more than eight characters long, and it should contain at least one alphabet, one number, and a symbol. So, I use the password `@packt000` for `jbossadmin`.

For the last option **Is this new user going to be used for one AS process to connect to another AS process?**, we choose **no**. In the later chapters, we'll create a user account for the remote server connection in the domain mode.

Using the web-based management console

Now let's try to use the EAP6 web management console in the standalone mode. Run `standalone.sh` in the `bin` folder of EAP6 to start up the server. Then, we access the web management console by its default address, `http://127.0.0.1:9990`. The management console will pop up a login window; enter the user account we've just created. The process is shown in the following screenshot:

After login, we can see the main window of the management console, as shown in the following screenshot:

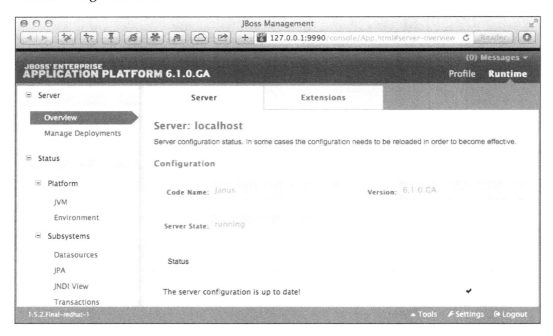

In the next section, we'll use the web-based management console to deploy a web application.

Deploying a project in the standalone mode

Now we can try to deploy a very simple web project named `cluster-demo1` into EAP6. It's a plain hello world project that contains a simple hello page, which shows the current time on the browser. To deploy this project into EAP6, we can click on the **Manage Deployments** tab in the management console and then click on **Add**.

Then, we choose `cluster-demo1.war` and click on **Next>>**.

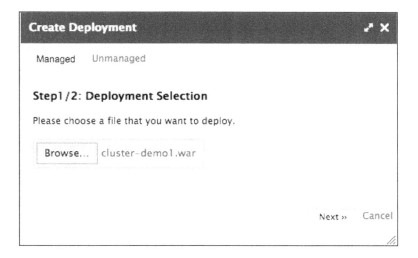

EAP6 will then ask us to verify the deployment names. We should accept the default name and click on **Save**. This process is shown in the following screenshot:

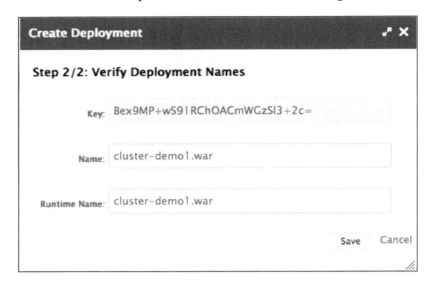

As the project has been deployed, the console will be redirected to the **Available Deployments** page. To start the deployed project, we need to select it and click on **En/Disable**. This process is shown in the following screenshot:

And we need to confirm to enable this project. This is done by clicking on **Confirm**, as shown in the following screenshot:

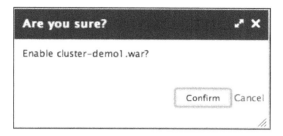

Finally, we can see that the project has started, as shown in the following screenshot:

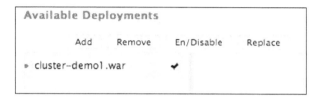

Now, if we check the server output from the console, we can see that `cluster-demo1.war` is deployed as follows:

```
18:55:46,557 INFO[org.jboss.as.server.deployment](MSC service
    thread 1-8)JBEAP6015876: Starting deployment of "cluster-
    demo1.war"(runtimename: "cluster-demo1.war")

18:55:46,622 INFO[org.jboss.web](ServerService Thread Pool --
    68)JBEAP6018210: Register webcontext: /cluster-demo1

18:55:46,638 INFO[org.jboss.as.server](HttpManagementService-
    threads - 21)JBEAP6018559: Deployed "cluster-demo1.war"
    (runtime-name : "cluster-demo1.war")
```

Now, let's have a look at `standalone.xml`. We can see that the description of this deployment has been added as follows:

```
<deployments>
  <deployment name="cluster-demo1.war" runtime-name="cluster-
    demo1.war">
    <content sha1="3afbf9c1d6fe967e0ff7eb190b862700b693e431"/>
  </deployment>
</deployments>
</server>
```

From the preceding code snippet, we can see that the content of the configuration file has been updated by the management console. Finally, let's check `standalone/data/content` as follows:

```
mini:jboss-eap-6.1weinanli$ tree standalone/data/content
standalone/data/content
└── 3a
└── fbf9c1d6fe967e0ff7eb190b862700b693e431
└── content
```

From the preceding code snippet, we can see that the contents of the deployed project is hashed and stored in the `standalone/data/content` directory.

Testing

Now we can try to access the deployed project to see if it's running correctly. In the following code snippet, I used the `curl` command to test the connection:

```
$ curl http://127.0.0.1:8080/cluster-demo1/index.jsp
<html>
  <body>
    <h2>Hello World!</h2>
    Hello! The time is now Wed Nov 20 15:50:22 CST 2013
</body>
</html>
```

As shown in the preceding process, we can see the hello page from the console output.

Deployment scanner

The standalone mode supports the traditional hot deployment used in the previous versions of JBoss AS. This method lets you put your copied project into a directory, and then JBoss EAP6 will scan the directory periodically to deploy the project copied into it. This function is supported by the deployment-scanner subsystem, which is defined in `standalone.xml` as follows:

```
<extension module="org.jboss.as.deployment-scanner"/>
```

The default setting for the subsystem in `standalone.xml` is given as follows:

```
<subsystem xmlns="urn:jboss:domain:deployment-scanner:1.1">
  <deployment-scanner path="deployments" relative
    to="jboss.server.base.dir" scan-interval="5000"/>
</subsystem>
```

It will scan the standalone deployments directory every 5 seconds and deploy the newly added projects. We can try to use the deployment scanner to deploy `cluster-demo1.war`. Before that, we need to undeploy this project from the web management console.

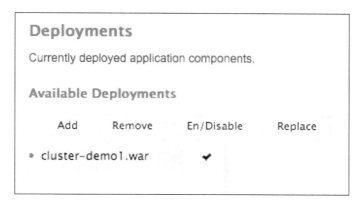

To undeploy the project, click on **En/Disable** and then click on **Remove**. After the project is undeployed, we can put `cluster-demo1.war` into `standalone/deployments` by using the following code:

```
$ mv cluster-demo1/target/cluster-demo1.war jboss-eap-
  6.1/standalone/deployments
```

Because the deployment scanner is set to scan this directory every 5 seconds, we will wait for a while and we'll see that the project is deployed from the server output as follows:

```
00:21:05,963 INFO[org.jboss.as.server](DeploymentScanner-
  threads - 2)JBAS018559: Deployed "cluster-demo1.war"(runtime-
  name : "cluster-demo1.war")
```

Now let's have a look at the `deployments` directory as follows:

```
README.txt                    cluster-demo1.war.deployed
cluster-demo1.warmod_cluster.sar
```

We can see that there is a new file named `cluster-demo1.war.deployed` that was created automatically. This is the marker file that is created by the deployment scanner to mark the status of our project. Now, let's delete this file by using the following code:

```
$ rm cluster-demo1.war.deployed
```

Wait a while and you can see the server output as follows:

```
00:26:21,289 INFO[org.jboss.as.server] (DeploymentScanner-
   threads - 2)JBEAP6018558: Undeployed"cluster-demo1.war"
   (runtime-name: "cluster-demo1.war")
```

Because we have deleted the `cluster-demo1.war.deployed` marker file, the scanner comes to know that we want to undeploy the project. So, it takes the action. Now let's check the `deployments` directory again by using the following code:

```
README.txt                      cluster-demo1.war.undeployed
cluster-demo1.warmod_cluster.sar
```

We can see that the scanner created another marker file called `cluster-demo1.war.undeployed`, which marks the `cluster-demo1.war` file as undeployed. If we delete the `cluster-demo1.war.undeployed` file by using the following code:

```
$ rm cluster-demo1.war.undeployed
```

Then the scanner will redeploy this project as follows:

```
00:29:41,499 INFO[org.jboss.as.server] (DeploymentScanner-
   threads - 2)JBEAP6018559: Deployed "cluster-demo1.war"
   (runtime-name : "cluster-demo1.war")
```

Now let's have a look at the `deployments` directory. We can see that the `cluster-demo1.war.deployed` marker file appeared again, as shown in the following code:

```
README.txt                      cluster-demo1.war.deployed
cluster-demo1.warmod_cluster.sar
```

 The deployment scanner can be used only in the standalone mode.

Introducing JBoss DMR

JBoss DMR is the cornerstone of the JBoss management module. All the management actions will be translated into the management commands that are encapsulated in the DMR format. The deployment actions used by the deployment scanner or the management console are all translated into the DMR commands at last. For example, when the deployment scanner wants to deploy a project into EAP6, it will send the following JSON-like DMR commands to the deployment module. The following is the trimmed text of the command:

```
[{
   "operation" =>"composite",
   "address" => [],
   "steps" => [
     {
       "operation" =>"add",
       "address" => [("deployment" =>"cluster-demo1.war")],
       "content" => [{
         "path" =>"deployments/cluster-demo1.war",
         "relative-to" =>"jboss.server.base.dir",
       }],
     },
     {
     "operation" =>"deploy",
     "address" => [("deployment" =>"cluster-demo1.war")]
     }
   ]
}]
```

We can see that the deployment scanner has sent a composition operation that contains two operations: add and deploy. This means that EAP6 will first add this project into its scope and then start it. In the web management console, we see that these two actions are separated — we first add a project into EAP6 and then we click on **En/Disable** to start it. Both the web management console and the command line interface send such kind of DMR commands to the deployment console.

Deploying a project in the domain mode

Now let's learn how to deploy a project in the domain mode. When JBoss EAP6 is running under the domain mode, multiple servers can form a server group. When we deploy a project into a server group, all the servers in this group will get the project deployed. First, let's start JBoss EAP6 in the domain mode by domain.sh. Then, we will access the management console address, http://127.0.0.1:9990. The management console under the domain mode is different from the standalone mode. It's shown in the following screenshot:

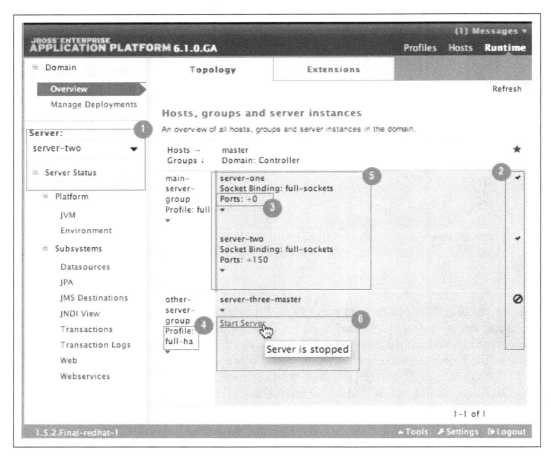

The following are some notes about the management console is shown in the preceding screenshot:

1. There is a **Server:** section in the sidebar where we can check all the servers in different server groups.

2. The marker indicates the running status of each server.

3. **Ports:** shows the port offsets of each server. Because these servers are running on the same machine, their ports must be offset to avoid confliction.

4. **Profile:** shows the profiles that the server group is bound to.

5. The servers that belong to the same group have the same colors on the management console.

6. We can start or stop a server in the management console.

There are two server groups by default. Let's check the main-server-group in the following section.

The main-server-group

We can see that the **main-server-group** includes two servers by default. Let's deploy `cluster-demo1.war` into these groups. Please make sure that these two servers are started. If they are not, we can use the **Start Server** function that is provided by the management console.

Now let's deploy `cluster-demo1.war`. First, we need to click on the **Management Deployments** tab that appears on the side bar. Then click on the **Content Repository** tab, and click on **Add**. This process is shown in the following screenshot:

Now we will choose `cluster-demo1.war`, as shown in the following screenshot:

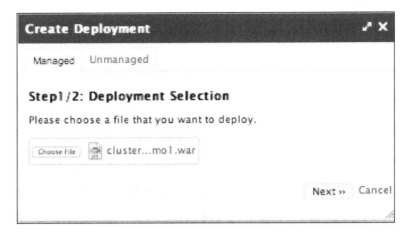

Now we click on **Next>>** and then click on **Save**. Then, we can see that the project is deployed into **Content Repository**. The result is shown in the following screenshot:

We can see that the deployment process in the domain mode is different from the standalone mode. We don't directly deploy a project into servers. Instead, we add it into **Content Repository** first and then deploy it to a server group. EAP6 will help us to deploy the project to all the servers in the group.

Now, let's deploy `cluster-demo1.war` to main-server-group. First click on the
Server Groups tab, and then click on **View>** of main-server-group, as shown in
the following screenshot:

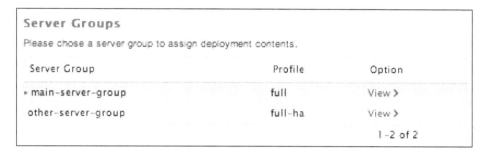

After clicking on **View>**, we enter the web page for **main-server-group**. Then, we
click on **Assign Name** and select `cluster-demo1.war` to save it. This is shown in
the following screenshot:

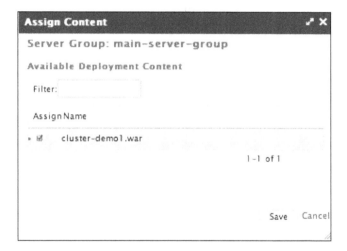

Finally, let's enable the project. Click on **En/Disable** and then click on **Confirm**, as shown in the following screenshot:

After confirming the deployment, the project should be deployed to **server-one** and **server-two**. Let's verify this.

Testing

Now let's try to access the two servers. Please note that the master-server is located at port 8080 and slave-server has a port offset of 150, so the web port is 8080+150 = 8230. The results are as follows:

```
mini:~ weinanli$ curl http://127.0.0.1:8080/cluster-demo1/index.jsp
<html>
<body>
<h2>Hello World!</h2>

Hello! The time is now Thu Oct 10 19:10:38 CST 2013
</body>
</html>
mini:~ weinanli$ curl http://127.0.0.1:8230/cluster-demo1/index.jsp
<html>
<body>
<h2>Hello World!</h2>

Hello! The time is now Thu Oct 10 19:10:45 CST 2013
</body>
</html>
mini:~ weinanli$
```

From the preceding screenshot, we can see that cluster-demo1.war is deployed in both the servers.

CLI Usages

The CLI provides a pure text environment for us to manage the EAP6 server, and it shares the same DMR model with the web management console. In this section, let's have a brief discussion about CLI usages.

Connecting to CLI

The command to start the CLI is `jboss-cli.sh`, which is located in the `bin` folder. Make sure that you have started EAP6 in the standalone mode. Let's run the CLI command now. This process is shown in the following code:

```
$ ./jboss-cli.sh
You are disconnected at the moment. Type 'connect' to connect to the
server or 'help' for the list of supported commands.
[disconnected /]
```

Now that we have entered the CLI console, the next step is to use the `connect` command to enter the management console as follows:

```
[disconnected /] connect localhost
[standalone@localhost:9999 /]
```

We have used the `connect` command to connect to the management console.

 You may have noticed that the CLI doesn't ask us to use the administrator account to log in. In the CLI, when we are connecting to the local EAP server, the authentication is bypassed.

As we have connected to the text management console, now let's learn some basic commands.

ls

The first command we'll learn is `ls`. It's similar to the `ls` command used in the shell environment. This command lists the resources in JBoss EAP6, as shown in the following screenshot:

```
                              1. java
[standalone@localhost:9999 /] ls
core-service
deployment
deployment-overlay
extension
```

We can see that the resources are organized in a tree structure. This is similar to a file system and we can use the ls command to check the contents of the resources as if it's a directory. For example, we can check the resources in a subsystem, as shown in the following screenshot:

```
 ● ○ ○                              1. java                               ⬈
[standalone@localhost:9999 /] ls subsystem
datasources          jmx                    resource-adapters
deployment-scanner   jpa                    sar
ee                   jsf                    security
ejb3                 logging                threads
infinispan           mail                   transactions
jaxrs                naming                 web
jca                  pojo                   webservices
jdr                  remoting               weld
[standalone@localhost:9999 /] ▊
```

cd

We can use the cd command to view resources as if they were directories. The usage is shown in the following screenshot:

```
 ● ○ ○                              2. java                               ⬈
[standalone@127.0.0.1:9999 /] cd subsystem
[standalone@127.0.0.1:9999 subsystem] cd ..
[standalone@127.0.0.1:9999 /] ▊
```

As shown in the preceding screenshot, we can use the cd command to traverse the resources.

Basic commands

The CLI provides a set of basic commands for us to use. We can press the *Tab* key twice to see a list of these commands, as shown in the following screenshot:

```
● ○ ○                        2. java                              ↗
[standalone@127.0.0.1:9999 /]
alias               echo-dmr              read-operation
batch               help                  reload
cd                  history               run-batch
clear               if                    shutdown
command             jdbc-driver-info      try
connect             ls                    undeploy
data-source         module                version
deploy              pwd                   xa-data-source
deployment-info     quit                  :
deployment-overlay  read-attribute
[standalone@127.0.0.1:9999 /] █
```

To understand the meaning of these commands, we can use the **--help** option after a command name. For example, if we want to understand the usage of connect, we can use the **--help** option as shown in the following screenshot:

```
● ○ ○                        2. java                              ↗
[standalone@127.0.0.1:9999 /] connect --help
SYNOPSIS

    connect [host][:port]

DESCRIPTION

    Connects to the controller on the specified host and port.
```

Among the basic commands, I want to specifically introduce echo-dmr and read-operation because they are the most frequently used ones.

echo-dmr

echo-dmr is used to build a DMR request for a command or operation. It is like a translator that translates the action into a DMR request. For example, if we want to understand how the deploy command constructs a DMR request, we can use echo-dmr to translate it:

```
[standalone@127.0.0.1:9999 /] echo-dmr deploy /cluster-
    demo1/cluster-demo1.war
{
    "operation" =>"composite",
    "address" => [],
    "steps" => [
        {
            "operation" =>"add",
```

```
             "address" => {"deployment" =>"cluster-demo1.war"},
             "content" => [{"bytes" => bytes {
                ...
             }}]
          },
          {
             "operation" =>"deploy",
             "address" => {"deployment" =>"cluster-demo1.war"}
          }
       ]
    }
```

It's very clear to see the underlying details of the deploy command from the preceding DMR request.

read-operation

In the CLI console, each resource has a set of operations that we can use on the resources. We can use read-operation to help us know the operations that could be operated on a resource. For example, if we want to find out what operations a web subsystem support, we can use read-operation as shown in the following screenshot:

```
⊙ ○ ○                              1. java
[standalone@localhost:9999 /] cd subsystem=web
[standalone@localhost:9999 subsystem=web] read-operation
add                          read-resource
read-attribute               read-resource-description
read-children-names          remove
read-children-resources      undefine-attribute
read-children-types          whoami
read-operation-description   write-attribute
read-operation-names
[standalone@localhost:9999 subsystem=web] []
```

For example, in the list shown in the preceding screenshot, we see an operation named **read-operation-names**. Let's try to use it as shown in the following screenshot:

```
●○○                            1. java                            ⤢
[standalone@localhost:9999 subsystem=web] :read-operation-names
{
    "outcome" => "success",
    "result" => [
        "add",
        "read-attribute",
        "read-children-names",
        "read-children-resources",
        "read-children-types",
        "read-operation-description",
        "read-operation-names",
        "read-resource",
        "read-resource-description",
        "remove",
        "undefine-attribute",
        "whoami",
        "write-attribute"
    ]
}
[standalone@localhost:9999 subsystem=web] []
```

We see that the read-operation-names operation is very similar to the
read-operation command; so what are their differences? Let's use echo-dmr
to check it, as shown in the following screenshot:

```
●○○                            1. java                            ⤢
[standalone@localhost:9999 subsystem=web] echo-dmr :read-operation-na
mes
{
    "address" => [("subsystem" => "web")],
    "operation" => "read-operation-names"
}
[standalone@localhost:9999 subsystem=web] echo-dmr read-operation
{
    "operation" => "read-operation-names",
    "address" => [("subsystem" => "web")]
}
[standalone@localhost:9999 subsystem=web] █
```

From the DMR level, we can see that their translated DMR request is exactly
the same.

The GUI

EAP CLI also supports a GUI interface, which is actually a swing application. We can start it by using the --gui option as follows:

```
$ ./jboss-cli.sh --gui
```

And the interface is shown in the following screenshot:

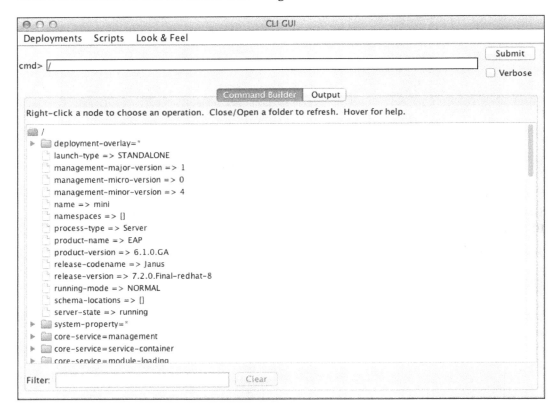

The GUI interface can also be used remotely. For example, if our management console is bound to a public IP address, we can access it from another machine with the GUI enabled by using the following command:

```
power:binweli$ ./jboss-cli.sh --controller=10.0.1.3:9999 --
    connect --gui
```

And the GUI will be started from the remote machine.

Deploying a project

Now let's use the CLI to deploy the project. The following command is used to do the deployment:

```
[standalone@localhost:9999 /] deploy /cluster-
  demo1/target/cluster-demo1.war
```

After the project is deployed, we can see it under `deployment` as follows:

```
[standalone@localhost:9999 /] ls deployment
cluster-demo1.war
```

Now, let's use the `undeploy` command to remove it as follows:

```
[standalone@localhost:9999 /] undeploy cluster-demo1.war
```

Checking the contents in `deployment`, we can see that it's removed as follows:

```
[standalone@localhost:9999 /] ls deployment
[standalone@localhost:9999 /]
```

Summary

In this chapter, we have learned how to add the administrator account into JBoss EAP6. We have also learned to use the management model to deploy the projects into EAP6 when it's running in the standalone mode or the domain mode. Then, we had a closer look at the design of the EAP6 management model and the DMR layer. With this knowledge, I hope you have a good understanding of JBoss EAP6's structure and grasp its basic usages. From the next chapter, we'll start to set an EAP6 cluster.

3
Setting Up a JBoss EAP6 Cluster

In the previous chapter, we have learned how to use the management console to deploy projects into JBoss EAP6 in both the standalone mode and domain mode. We also saw that the domain mode has helped us a lot when we needed to manage multiple servers. It achieved this goal by centralizing the management task into a domain controller.

The domain mode provided by EAP6 is a good support to help us set up our cluster, but it's still not the cluster itself. As we have seen in *Chapter 2*, *Using JBoss EAP6*, though servers are managed in a server group, they do not form a cluster. For the servers to form a cluster, we need to perform the following two tasks:

- Setting up the EAP6 servers properly to make sure the components related with clustering are all running in correct status
- Setting up a load balancer so that user requests can be dispatched to the different EAP6 servers contained in the cluster

In this chapter, we'll focus on the first task.

Designing a cluster

In the previous chapter, we have seen that EAP6 has provided two server groups in `domain.xml`. One is called **main-server-group** and the other is called **other-server-group**. In this chapter, we'll use the other-server-group to set the cluster, because it's using the `full-ha` profile, and this profile contains all the components we'll use to set up the cluster.

With a cluster, we can distribute the request load to multiple servers. With the EAP6 domain management function, we can deploy a project into multiple EAP6 servers in the management console of the domain controller.

We will use three machines to set up a cluster in this book. Two of them will be used to run the EAP6 servers, and one of them will be used to run the load balancer. In this chapter, we will use two machines to run the EAP6 servers.

 You can also use virtualization to have all of them running in a single physical box. Just make sure they have independent IP addresses that can communicate with one another, and the firewalls are turned off.

The deployment process is shown in following diagram:

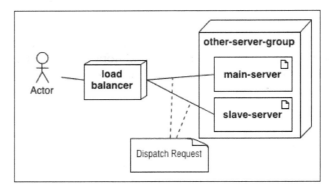

In this chapter, we'll use two machines and install EAP6 on both of them, and we'll talk about the load balancer in the next chapter. The deployment diagram of two EAP6 servers is shown in the following diagram:

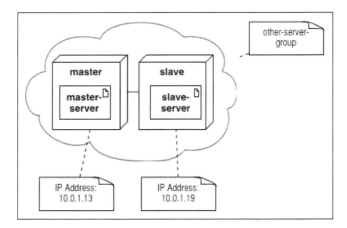

The two machines are called **master** and **slave**. I have put the IP addresses of these two servers into the diagram for your reference. These addresses are used in my local environment. In the diagram, the EAP6 server on **master** will be configured as a domain controller, and the EAP6 server running on **slave** will accept the management of **master**.

In `domain/configuration/host.xml`, EAP6 has provided us with a default server that belongs to other-server-group. We'll rename this server on **master** as `master-server`, and rename the one on **slave** as `slave-server`.

In the EAP6 domain mode, each server instance is running in its own JVM process. The following are the processes that will be running on **master**:

```
/usr/bin/java -D[Process Controller]
/usr/bin/java -D[Host Controller]
/usr/bin/java -D[Server:master-server]
```

The following are the processes that will be running on **slave**:

```
/usr/bin/java -D[Process Controller]
/usr/bin/java -D[Host Controller]
/usr/bin/java -D[Server:slave-server]
```

The host controller running on **master** will act as the domain controller; the host controller running on **slave** will accept the management from the domain controller. In addition, both master-server and slave-server belong to other-server-group. When we deploy a project into other-server-group, the project will be deployed to both the servers, because they belong to the same server group, even though they are running on different machines and with different JVMs.

Setting up a server group

In this section we'll start doing some configurations in EAP6. As we know, there are two server groups already set up for us in JBoss EAP6:

- main-server-group
- other-server-group

And in *Chapter 2, Using JBoss EAP6*, we have played with main-server-group. In this chapter we'll use other-server-group.

The main-server-group versus other-server-group

The major difference is that they are using two different profiles. You can see this in `domain.xml`:

```
<server-group name="main-server-group" profile="full">...
<server-group name="other-server-group" profile="full-ha">...
```

As shown in the preceding configuration, we don't define different profiles into different configuration files in the domain mode. Instead it's defined in different profile sections in `domain.xml`.

Server configuration

Now let's start configuring our server group. Because we need to configure two EAP6 instances on two different machines, let's go through them one by one. Let's start with **master**.

Setting up master

The EAP6 on **master** will be used as a domain controller. Let's start configuring it.

Configuring host.xml

The first thing we should do is set the host name in `domain/configuration/host.xml`. Let's set the hostname to `master`:

```
<host name="master" xmlns="urn:jboss:domain:1.4">
```

Then let's set the server group and server. Because we don't need to use main-server-group and its servers in this chapter, it's better to turn them off to save some system resources. Open `host.xml` and set the `auto-start` option of **server-one** and **server-two** to `false`:

```
<server name="server-one" group="main-server-group" auto-start="false">...
<server name="server-two" group="main-server-group" auto-start="false">...
```

The next time we start the EAP6 in the domain mode, these two servers won't start. Then let's rename `server-three` as `master-server` and set its `auto-start` to `true`:

```
<server name="master-server" group="other-server-group" auto-start="true">
  <socket-bindings port-offset="250"/>
</server>
```

Please note that the port offset of `master-server` is `250`, and we'll use it to calculate the serving ports of `master-server`. The next thing we should do is to change the binding addresses of multiple sockets to public IP addresses. Because we'll use two EAP6 servers on two different machines to form a server group, we need to bind sockets to proper addresses to make sure they can communicate with each other.

```
<interfaces>
  <interface name="management">
  <inet-address value="$
    {jboss.bind.address.management:10.0.1.13}"/>
  </interface>
  <interface name="public">
    <inet-address value="${jboss.bind.address:10.0.1.13}"/>
  </interface>
  <interface name="unsecure">
  <inet-address value="$
    {jboss.bind.address.unsecure:10.0.1.13}"/>
  </interface>
</interfaces>
```

Please note that the **slave** server will connect to the master's management interface to accept its management, so it should also be bound to public address as shown in the previous code snippet. We'll cover **slave** configuration in later sections.

The public address here means the IP address other than the loopback address. It should be an internal IP address only accessible from LAN. In a real-world scenario, the management interface won't be public. They would use only an internal network because of security reasons. So we usually put all the EAP6 servers in a LAN, and only open the load balancer to the public, and let it proxy user requests to the internal network. We'll discuss this in the next chapter.

Adding a user account for slave server

The two servers (master-server and slave-server) will be managed by the domain, and we need to use host controllers to connect to the domain. The communication between the two host controllers needs to be authenticated. If slave-server wants to connect to the domain controller, we need to set up a user account for the connection, which is enforced by the security requirement of JBoss EAP6.

We'll use `add-user.sh` in the `bin` directory to create a user for slave. The process is shown in the following screenshot:

```
● ○ ○                              10. bash
master:bin $ ./add-user.sh

What type of user do you wish to add?
 a) Management User (mgmt-users.properties)
 b) Application User (application-users.properties)
(a): a

Enter the details of the new user to add.
Realm (ManagementRealm) :
Username : slave
Password :
Re-enter Password :
About to add user 'slave' for realm 'ManagementRealm'
Is this correct yes/no? yes
Added user 'slave' to file '/packt/jboss-eap-6.1/standalone/configuration/mgmt-u
sers.properties'
Added user 'slave' to file '/packt/jboss-eap-6.1/domain/configuration/mgmt-users
.properties'
Is this new user going to be used for one AS process to connect to another AS pr
ocess?
e.g. for a slave host controller connecting to the master or for a Remoting conn
ection for server to server EJB calls.
yes/no? yes
To represent the user add the following to the server-identities definition <sec
ret value="QHBhY2t0MDAw" />
master:bin $ ▯
```

The following is the summary of the user we've created:

- The type of user is **Management User**
- The user name is **slave**
- The user password is set to **@packt000**
- The user belongs to **ManagementRealm**
- **Is this new user going to be used for one AS process to connect to another AS process** is set to **yes**

The last point is important; we have set this user to be used for the AS process connection, and a secret value is generated for this user:

```
<secret value="QHBhY2t0MDAw" />
```

This is the secret value that we'll need for `slave-server` to connect to `master-server`. We need to enter this secret value into **slave** EAP6. Another important thing is that the username here must be the same as the `name` attribute in `host.xml` of **slave** EAP6. If you don't follow this rule, you will receive the following error message when you try to start EAP6 on **slave**:

```
[Host Controller] 22:31:40,341 DEBUG
  [org.jboss.remoting.remote.client] (Remoting "slave:
  MANAGEMENT" read-1) Client received authentication
  rejected for mechanism DIGEST-MD5
[Host Controller] 22:31:40,344 ERROR
  [org.jboss.remoting.remote.connection] (Remoting "slave:
  MANAGEMENT" read-1) JBREM000200: Remote connection failed:
  javax.security.sasl.SaslException: Authentication failed:
  all available authentication mechanisms failed
```

So this rule is enforced by EAP6.

Setting up HornetQ

There is one more step to configure the **master** server. Open `domain.xml` and find the security setting of **HornetQ**:

```
<profile name="full-ha">
  <subsystem xmlns="urn:jboss:domain:messaging:1.3">
    <hornetq-server>
    <cluster-password>${jboss.messaging.
      cluster.password:CHANGE ME!!}
</cluster-password>
  . . .
```

 Both the `full-ha` and `full` profiles in `domain.xml` contains the settings of `hornetq-server`. Please make sure you are editing the configuration under the `full-ha` profile.

Change the preceding setting to the following:

```
<hornetq-server>
  <cluster-user>foo</cluster-password>
  <cluster-password>bar</cluster-password>
</hornetq-server>
```

If you feel this is not very useful, you can also disable it:

```
<hornetq-server>
  <security-enabled>false</security-enabled>
</hornetq-server>
```

We won't cover the topics of HornetQ in this book. We just configure it properly to make sure the EAP6 server could start correctly.

Setting up slave

Now let's configure EAP6 on **slave**. Because it will accept the management from **master** EAP6, domain.xml on this server becomes useless. We just need to configure host.xml. Now let's have a look at it.

Configuring host.xml

Similar to the configuration on **master** EAP6, we first need to configure the name of the host:

```
<host name="slave" xmlns="urn:jboss:domain:1.4">
```

As noted in the *Configuring host.xml* section of *Setting up a master*, the name here must be the same as the username of the account we have added in **master** EAP6. Then we need to assign the secret value to ManagementRealm:

```
<security-realm name="ManagementRealm">
  <server-identities>
    <secret value="QHBhY2t0MDMDAw"/>
  </server-identities>
  . . .
</security-realm name="ManagementRealm">
```

Then host controller of **slave** will use this secret value for authentication. The next step is to set up domain-controller:

```
<domain-controller>
  <remote host="10.0.1.13" port="9999"
    security-realm="ManagementRealm"/>
</domain-controller>
```

As shown before, the **slave** EAP6 will connect to the **master** EAP6 and use it as the domain controller.

 Remember that 10.0.1.13 is the IP address of **master**, while 10.0.1.19 is the address of **slave**.

The next step is to bind the interfaces of **slave** EAP6 to proper IP addresses so that the **master** EAP6 can communicate with it:

```
<interfaces>
  <interface name="management">
    <inet-address value="${jboss.bind.
    address.management:127.0.0.1}"/>
  </interface>
  <interface name="public">
    <inet-address value="${jboss.bind.address:10.0.1.19}"/>
  </interface>
  <interface name="unsecure">
    <inet-address value="$
      {jboss.bind.address.unsecure:10.0.1.19}"/>
  </interface>
</interfaces>
```

Please note that we didn't change the binding for the management interface. Because the domain controller will undertake the management work, the local management on **slave** won't be used. So let's just leave it unchanged.

Next we also turn off server-one and server-two to save some resources:

```
<server name="server-one" group="main-server-group"
  auto-start="false">
<server name="server-two" group="main-server-group"
  auto-start="false">
```

Finally let's rename server-three as slave-server and set auto-start to true:

```
<server name="slave-server" group="other-server-group"
  auto-start="true">
```

That's all we need to configure for slave EAP6.

Configuring domain.xml on slave

The domain.xml on **slave** EAP6 is not used because the **master** EAP6 is acting as a domain controller and it will take the management tasks.

Testing the server group

Now that we have properly set up the **master** and **slave** EAP6, it's time to run them for testing.

Running master

First let's run the following command on **master** EAP6:

```
$ ./domain.sh
```

After the master server starts, let's check the server output shown in the following screenshot:

```
○ ○ ○                          6. bash                            ⤢
[Host Controller] 01:11:35,366 INFO  [org.jboss.as.host.controller] (
Controller Boot Thread) JBAS010922: Starting server master-server
[Host Controller] 01:11:36,629 INFO  [org.jboss.as.domain.controller.
mgmt] (Remoting "mini:MANAGEMENT" task-4) JBAS010920: Server [Server:
master-server] registered using connection [Channel ID 5b7d5ffb (inbo
und) of Remoting connection 226c4923 to /10.0.1.13:55502]
[Host Controller] 01:11:36,722 INFO  [org.jboss.as.host.controller] (
server-registration-threads - 1) JBAS010919: Registering server maste
r-server
```

In the preceding screenshot we can see that `master-server` has started. Then we can see that the management interface and admin console have also started. The log output is shown in the following screenshot:

```
○ ○ ○                          6. bash                            ⤢
[Host Controller] 01:11:36,944 INFO  [org.jboss.as] (Controller Boot
Thread) JBAS015961: Http management interface listening on http://10.
0.1.13:9990/management
[Host Controller] 01:11:36,945 INFO  [org.jboss.as] (Controller Boot
Thread) JBAS015951: Admin console listening on http://10.0.1.13:9990
```

Now we can see that the multiple components related with cluster have started:

- The JGroups subsystem has started.
- The AJP connector has started. Load balancers will use it for proxy requests. We'll cover this topic in the next chapter.
- The HTTP connector has started. Because the port offset for `master-server` is `250` and the HTTP port is bound to `8080`, 8080+250 = `8330`.
- `mod_cluster` has started. We'll learn about `mod_cluster` in *Chapter 5, Load Balancing with mod_cluster*.

The described process is shown in the following screenshot:

```
⬤ ⚪ ⚪                        6. bash
[Server:master-server] 01:11:37,140 INFO  [org.jboss.as.clustering.jgroups]
(ServerService Thread Pool -- 50) JBAS010260: Activating JGroups subsystem.
[Server:master-server] 01:11:37,480 INFO  [org.apache.coyote.ajp] (MSC servi
ce thread 1-12) JBWEB003046: Starting Coyote AJP/1.3 on ajp-/10.0.1.13:8259
[Server:master-server] 01:11:37,480 INFO  [org.apache.coyote.http11] (MSC se
rvice thread 1-7) JBWEB003001: Coyote HTTP/1.1 initializing on : http-/10.0.
1.13:8330
[Server:master-server] 01:11:37,512 INFO  [org.jboss.modcluster] (ServerServ
ice Thread Pool -- 62) MODCLUSTER000001: Initializing mod\_cluster ${project
.version} [Server:master-server] 01:11:37,530 INFO  [org.jboss.modcluster] (
ServerService Thread Pool -- 62) MODCLUSTER000032: Listening to proxy advert
isements on /224.0.1.105:23364
```

Running slave

Now let's start the **slave** server by using domain.sh. Its host controller will try to connect to the remote domain controller on **master**. After the **slave** server starts, we could check the console output from **master** EAP6 to confirm that the **slave** has been registered:

```
[Host Controller] 01:22:48,527 INFO  [org.jboss.as.domain]
   (slave-request-threads - 1) JBAS010918: Registered remote
   slave host "slave", JBoss EAP 6.1.0.GA (AS 7.2.0.Final-redhat-8)
```

Checking the server status

Now let's access the web manage console on **master** EAP6 at http://master:9990.

After logging in with the account jbossadmin, we can check the status of master-server and slave-server. Here is their status:

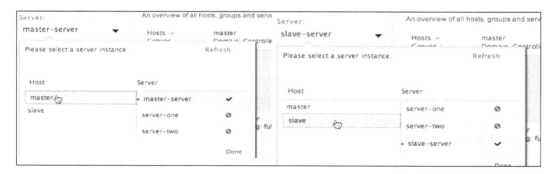

As shown in the screenshots, both **master** and **slave** are shown in the management console. That means the domain controller is managing all the servers. Now let's go to **slave** and try to access its management console. The result is as follows:

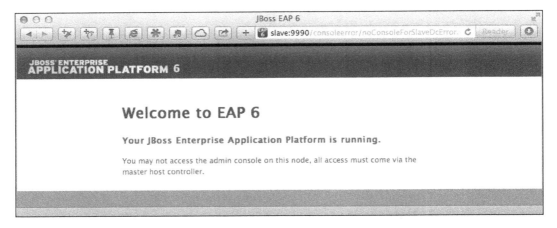

We can see that **slave** EAP6 is now under the management of the domain controller.

Project deployment

Now let's deploy `cluster-demo1` into `other-server-group`.

Deploying a project to other-server-group

In the previous chapter we already learned how to deploy a project into the server group, so I will briefly describe the process here:

1. Log in to the management console of **master** EAP6.
2. Click on **Manage Deployments** in the sidebar.
3. Click on **Add** under the **Content Repository** tab and add **cluster-demo1.war**.
4. Follow the instructions and save the deployment.
5. Click on the **Server Groups** tab.
6. Click on **View** of **other-server-group**.
7. Click on **Assign** and select **cluster-demo1.war**.
8. Save the deployment and click on **En/Disable** to start the **cluster-demo1.war** file.

If everything goes fine, you should see the server output from both **master** and **slave**. The following is the output on master:

```
[Server:master-server] 23:31:58,223 INFO  [org.jboss.as.server] (host-
controller-connection-threads - 3) JBAS018559: Deployed "cluster-
demo1.war" (runtime-name : "cluster-demo1.war")
```

The following is the output on **slave**:

```
[Server:slave-server] 23:31:58,246 INFO  [org.jboss.as.server] (host-
controller-connection-threads - 3) JBAS018559: Deployed "cluster-
demo1.war" (runtime-name : "cluster-demo1.war")
```

With the help of the domain mode, the project is deployed into two servers that belong to the same group. Now we can verify that the project has been deployed to these two servers by using **cURL**:

```
⊝ ○ ○                        5. bash
$ curl http://master:8330/cluster-demo1/index.jsp
<html>
<body>
<h2>Hello World!</h2>

Hello! The time is now Tue Nov 19 05:31:09 CST 2013
</body>
</html>
$ curl http://slave:8330/cluster-demo1/index.jsp
<html>
<body>
<h2>Hello World!</h2>

Hello! The time is now Tue Nov 19 05:31:13 CST 2013
</body>
</html>
$ []
```

Clustering with the standalone mode

In the preceding sections we saw that the domain mode provides us a central place to manage our servers. The question is, do we need to use the domain mode to build an EAP6 cluster? The answer is, not necessarily.

Using the standalone mode to build a cluster is perfectly fine. We just need to enable the relative subsystems that are needed for building the cluster. And EAP6 has provided us a set of configurations in the standalone mode. The *-ha.xml files contain the profiles for clustering. We can use them during the startup. The following is the command:

```
$ ./standalone.sh -c standalone-full-ha.xml
```

Here are some disadvantages of using the standalone mode in the clustering environment:

- We have to configure each EAP6 server separately
- There is no centralized point to manage these servers

That means we must deploy the project to each EAP6 server separately, and make sure they are in sync during redeployment. In addition, if we run multiple standalone EAP6 servers on the same machine, we have to carefully set the offset for all the ports to prevent them from conflicting with one another. Apart from these disadvantages, there are some advantages of the standalone mode for clustering:

- You can configure each server independently. For example, we can turn off the HornetQ subsystem on server A, and enable it on servers B and C.
- The server running in the standalone mode can be debugged easily. In the domain mode, EAP6 will spawn multiple processes: a process-controller process, a host-controller process, and multiple server processes (each server instance runs in its own JVM space), and it will add some difficulties for debugging.

Summary

In this chapter we have looked at the configuration of the EAP6 cluster, and we have set up two EAP6 servers running in the domain mode to form a server group. Nevertheless, we haven't finished all the work of building a cluster: Now we have two EAP6 servers running independently, and we still need a load balancer to dispatch user requests to these two servers. In the next chapter, let's focus on setting up a load balancer.

4
Load Balancing with mod_jk

In the previous chapter, we set up two EAP6 servers running in domain mode with the `full-ha` profile. In this chapter, let's set up a load balancer that could dispatch user requests to these two EAP6 servers.

The load balancer we use in this chapter is called mod_jk provided by the Apache community. It's easy to use and yet very powerful. The following diagram shows how it works:

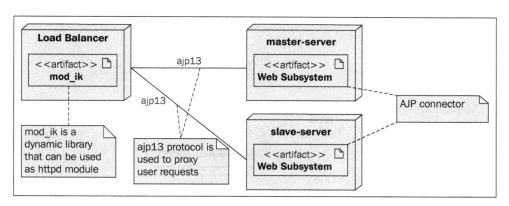

The following are some notes regarding the previous diagram:

- mod_jk is a dynamic library that can be used as an Apache httpd module. In this chapter, we'll learn how to use it.
- AJP13 is a binary protocol used by mod_jk to proxy user requests to JBoss EAP6 servers. AJP13 stands for Apache JServ Protocol 1.3 and is widely used by Tomcat, Jetty, and other web servers.

- When Apache httpd receives user requests, the mod_jk module will wrap the HTTP request into AJP13 format and pass it to JBoss EAP6, and the AJP connector in JBoss EAP6 will receive the proxy request from httpd. Then, EAP6 will process the request and send the response back to Apache httpd. Finally, Apache httpd will process the AJP response from JBoss EAP6 and transform it into the real HTTP response and send it back to a user.

In practice, we usually bind the load balancer to the public IP address so it can listen to user requests from the Internet and put the EAP6 worker nodes in the local network. In addition, we should also bind a local IP address for the load balancer so it can communicate with EAP6 servers. Users just need to communicate with the load balancer to access the service, and they don't need to understand the architecture behind the load balancer. In addition, exposing the internal architecture of a cluster to the public is unnecessary and could introduce a potential security risk.

Preparing a machine to install Apache httpd

As we have seen in the previous chapter, our cluster deployment structure will be as follows:

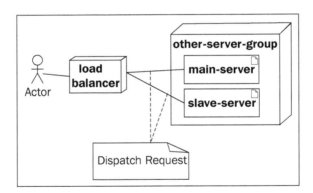

We have configured the two EAP6 servers in the previous chapter. Now, we will install Apache httpd and mod_jk on a machine as the load balancer, and let's call it lb. This machine will have two IP addresses:

- A public IP address that will serve user requests
- A local IP address that can communicate with JBoss EAP6 servers in the local network

If your computer has just one local IP address, you can use it to serve both user requests and to communicate with EAP6 servers. But in practice, we usually hide the clustering architecture behind a firewall.

Compiling and installing Apache httpd

Now, let's learn how to compile and install Apache httpd. You may ask why we need to compile the Apache httpd by ourselves. There are multiple reasons. Usually, the httpd is provided by different platforms that have different versions and different configurations. For example, if you are using Ubuntu Linux and I'm using MacOS, our httpd versions will be different and our configurations of httpd will also be different.

In practice, compiling httpd, mod_jk, and mod_cluster is also common. This is because sometimes the newer versions of mod_jk and mod_cluster are released in the source code format before the binary format. So, we need to build them by ourselves.

Downloading httpd

First, let's download the source code of Apache httpd from its website. We'll use the httpd 2.2.x in this book. This branch is currently the most stable version to work with mod_jk and mod_cluster. At the time of this writing, the newest version in 2.2.x branch is httpd 2.2.25, so let's use this to build our load balancer. Please note that the versions of httpd, mod_jk, and mod_cluster are very important, so please stick to the versions we used in this book or you may waste time on some bugs. You can download httpd 2.2.25 from `http://archive.apache.org/dist/httpd/httpd-2.2.25.tar.gz`.

After downloading it, please extract it to a directory that you have full access to. I've extracted it to `/packt/`:

```
$ pwd
/packt
$ tar zxvf httpd-2.2.25.tar.gz
...
$ ls
httpd-2.2.25         httpd-2.2.25.tar.gz
```

Because we'll use the absolute path in some situations, please don't put the source in a very deep path, or you'll create unnecessary difficulties when referring to your absolute path.

Compiling httpd

To compile httpd, first let's have a look at the contents of the sources shown as follows:

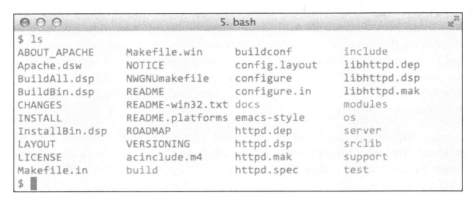

```
$ ls
ABOUT_APACHE     Makefile.win      buildconf        include
Apache.dsw       NOTICE            config.layout    libhttpd.dep
BuildAll.dsp     NWGNUmakefile     configure        libhttpd.dsp
BuildBin.dsp     README            configure.in     libhttpd.mak
CHANGES          README-win32.txt  docs             modules
INSTALL          README.platforms  emacs-style      os
InstallBin.dsp   ROADMAP           httpd.dep        server
LAYOUT           VERSIONING        httpd.dsp        srclib
LICENSE          acinclude.m4      httpd.mak        support
Makefile.in      build             httpd.spec       test
$
```

In the contents, there is a file called `configure` that will detect your system settings and generate the build script `Makefile` for you. Let's run it first:

```
./configure --prefix=/packt/httpd \
    --with-mpm=worker \
    --enable-mods-shared=most \
    --enable-maintainer-mode \
    --with-expat=builtin \
    --enable-ssl \
    --enable-proxy \
    --enable-proxy-http \
    --enable-proxy-ajp \
    --disable-proxy-balancer
```

As shown in the previous code snippet, we have provided several options to the `configure` script. Let's check them one by one:

`prefix=/packt/httpd`	The `prefix` option defines the binaries install location.
`with-mpm=worker`	MPM is the httpd process engine. The `worker` engine currently works stable with httpd 2.2.x, so we'll use it.
`enable-mods-shared=most`	This option will compile the modules into the shared library. If we don't enable it, the modules will be compiled as a static-linked library and we cannot disable them separately with the `LoadModule` directive in `httpd.conf` later.

enable-maintainer-mode	An option to control the Automake tool.
with-expat=builtin	Expat is an XML parser library written in C.
enable-ssl	The SSL library will be needed in the chapter that concerns the SSL support in the clustering environment.
enable-proxy	The proxy library is a dependency of mod_cluster. We'll learn about mod_cluster in the next chapter.
enable-proxy-http	proxy-http is needed by mod_cluster.
enable-proxy-ajp	proxy-ajp is needed by mod_jk and mod_cluster.
disable-proxy-balancer	proxy-balancer conflicts with mod_cluster, so we must disable it.

After understanding the meaning of these options, please run the `configure` command with the preceding options. Now let's run `make` to compile httpd:

```
httpd-2.2.25$ make
Making all in srclib
Making all in pcre
...
```

Wait a few minutes and the compiling should finish.

Installing httpd

After compiling it, use the following command to install the compiled binaries:

```
httpd-2.2.25$ make install
Making install in srclib
Making install in pcre
...
mkdir /packt/httpd
mkdir /packt/httpd/modules
...
Installing man pages and online manual
mkdir /packt/httpd/man
...
```

As we can see, the compiled binaries are installed in the directory we've set the `--prefix` option. For me, it is `/packt/httpd`.

Starting httpd

Now, let's try to start httpd to see if it's installed correctly. Go to the `bin` directory of your installed httpd and run the following command:

```
httpd/bin$ sudo ./httpd -k start -f /packt/httpd/conf/httpd.conf
```

We have used the `-k` option with the start command to tell httpd to start and the `-f` option with the full path of `httpd.conf` to make sure that the httpd server is using the configuration file we installed.

We are using the `sudo` command because we need the root access to bind the httpd service to port 80. If the server starts successfully, it will show some warnings:

```
httpd: Could not reliably determine the server's fully qualified
    domain name, using localhost.local for ServerName
```

The warning is caused by the missing config of `ServerName` in `httpd.conf`. We'll configure it correctly later. Now, let's check the log output. Go to the logs directory and check `error_log`:

```
httpd/logs$ tail -f error_log
. . .
[Thu Oct 03 15:19:18 2013] [notice] Apache/2.2.25 (Unix)
    mod_ssl/2.2.25 OpenSSL/1.0.1c DAV/2 configured -- resuming
    normal operations
```

The `error_log` file can help us to check if there are any errors when you run the httpd server. Here, we have used the tail command to check the tail contents of this log, and the `-f` option will keep updating the contents of `error_log` into the console. So, please keep the console window open; we can always check for any error when we are playing around with httpd. Now, we can use the cURL command to test the httpd service:

```
$ curl http://localhost
<html><body><h1>It works!</h1></body></html>
```

As we can see, the HTTP service is up. Now, let's stop the httpd server and do some basic configurations in `httpd.conf`.

Stopping httpd

The command to stop httpd is similar to the command that starts it; only replace `start` with `stop`:

```
sudo httpd -k stop -f /packt/httpd/conf/httpd.conf
```

From `error_log`, we can see that the server has stopped:

```
[Thu Oct 03 16:23:59 2013] [notice] caught SIGTERM, shutting down
```

Configuring httpd

Now, let's do some basic configuration for httpd. The first step is to back up your original `httpd.conf`:

```
httpd/conf$ cp httpd.conf httpd.conf.orig
```

It's a good habit to keep an original copy of your configuration; in case we mess it up, we can restore it later. The next step is to open `http.conf` with your favorite editor and find the following code line:

```
Listen 80
```

We need to change it for httpd to listen to the public address:

```
Listen 172.16.123.1:80
```

I've configured this IP address on the machine lb, and it will be used to listen to user requests. Note that it's a good habit to bind httpd to specific IP addresses and ports to prevent potential security risks. Besides the public IP address, the machine lb also has a local IP address, `10.0.1.32`. The former one will be used for public access from users; the latter one sits in the same LAN with the two EAP6 servers. If your machine doesn't have two IP addresses, it's okay to just use the single address for both purposes. Just keep in mind, in practice, we usually put the clustering architecture behind a firewall.

Now let's go to the next step. We need to find the following line:

```
#ServerName www.example.com:80
```

Let's put our own server name under this line:

```
ServerName lb
```

That's all we need to configure in `httpd.conf` for now. Let's save the configuration and quit editing. Next, we need to make sure the hostname lb is mapped to our public IP address. For a Linux-like environment, we can put the mapping in `/etc/hosts`. Open the `httpd.conf` file and add the following line at the bottom:

```
172.16.123.1 lb
```

After saving the configuration file, we can use the `ping` command to test the hostname:

```
$ ping -c 3 lb
PING lb (172.16.123.1): 56 data bytes
64 bytes from 172.16.123.1: icmp_seq=0 ttl=64 time=0.036 ms
64 bytes from 172.16.123.1: icmp_seq=1 ttl=64 time=0.079 ms
64 bytes from 172.16.123.1: icmp_seq=2 ttl=64 time=0.087 ms
```

Now, let's start httpd to check our configuration:

```
sudo httpd -k start -f /packt/httpd/conf/httpd.conf
```

If you still keep the tail `-f logs/error_log` console opened, you can check it immediately to see if there are any errors during startup. If everything goes fine, we can access the httpd server by the hostname now:

```
$ curl http://lb
<html><body><h1>It works!</h1></body></html>
```

As shown in the previous code snippet, the hostname lb is bound to the httpd server. In addition, during the httpd server startup, note that the warning **httpd: Could not reliably determine the server's fully qualified domain name** disappeared. That's because we have configured `ServerName` in `httpd.conf`.

As we have configured httpd, the next step is to learn to use mod_jk.

Compiling and installing mod_jk

The full name of mod_jk is Apache Tomcat Connector. It was originally designed to proxy HTTP requests from httpd to Tomcat, but as it is a standard AJP connector, it can be used on web containers that support the AJP protocol. Because JBoss EAP6 supports the AJP13 protocol, we can use mod_jk as its connector.

 To save some typing, in the following text I'll use JK to refer to mod_jk.

Installing JK

The download page of JK is at http://tomcat.apache.org/download-connectors.cgi.

At the time of this writing, the newest version is 1.2.37, and it's the version we'll use in this book. Please download the 1.2.37 source bundle from the previously mentioned website and unzip it after download. After all this is finished, let's have a look at the contents of the source package:

```
tomcat-connectors-1.2.37-src$ ls
HOWTO-RELEASE.txt  conf          support
LICENSE            docs          tools
NOTICE             jkstatus      xdocs
README.txt         native
```

As we can see, mod_jk contains many components, but we only need to build the codes in the native directory. Let's go into this directory and run the `configure` script inside:

```
$ ./configure --with-apxs=/packt/httpd/bin/apxs
```

Please note that we have been provided with the `--with-apxs` option to configure, because during the building process, it needs the httpd binaries. The configuration process is shown as follows:

```
tomcat-connectors-1.2.37-src/native$ ./configure --with-apxs=/packt/
httpd/bin/apxs
checking build system type...
checking host system type...
...
config.status: executing depfiles commands
After configure process finished, run make to compile it:
tomcat-connectors-1.2.37-src/native$ make
libtool: install: warning: remember to run `libtool --finish /packt/
httpd/modules'
...
Making all in common
Making all in apache-2.0
make[1]: Nothing to be done for `all'.
```

Now let's install it by running `make install`:

```
tomcat-connectors-1.2.37-src/native$ make install
Making install in apache-2.0

Installing files to Apache Modules Directory...
cp .libs/mod_jk.so /packt/httpd/modules/mod_jk.so
chmod 755 /packt/httpd/modules/mod_jk.so

Please be sure to arrange /packt/httpd/conf/httpd.conf...
```

I have trimmed the log output and just left the important parts. From the previous log, we can see that the compiled shared binary mod_jk.so has been copied to /packt/httpd/modules/. Because we have set the httpd path using the --with-apxs option, during the installation process, the build script knows where to put the compiled binary.

At the end of the log, JK has reminded us to configure httpd.conf to enable it. In the following section, we will perform this task.

Configuring JK

In the JK source, there is a directory called conf. In this directory, JK has provided us some sample configuration files that we can refer to:

```
$ ls /packt/tomcat-connectors-1.2.37-src/conf
httpd-jk.conf              workers.properties
uriworkermap.properties    workers.properties.minimal
```

Let's copy these files into httpd. First, let us create a new directory called conf.d in httpd:

```
/packt/httpd$ mkdir conf.d
```

Then, let's copy the configuration file from JK source to conf.d:

```
$ cp /packt/tomcat-connectors-1.2.37-src/conf/httpd-jk.conf
  /packt/httpd/conf.d/
```

We want httpd to load conf.d/httpd-jk.conf during startup. To achieve this goal, please open conf/httpd.conf and find many lines starting with LoadModule. At the bottom of these LoadModule directives, let's put a new code line:

```
Include conf.d/*.conf
```

The modification is shown in the following screenshot:

```
000                            2. ssh                             ⟲
LoadModule userdir_module modules/mod_userdir.so
LoadModule alias_module modules/mod_alias.so
LoadModule rewrite_module modules/mod_rewrite.so

Include conf.d/*.conf▯

<IfModule !mpm_netware_module>
<IfModule !mpm_winnt_module>
#
# If you wish httpd to run as a different user or group, you must ru\
n
# httpd as root initially and it will switch.
#
# User/Group: The name (or #number) of the user/group to run httpd a\
s.
# It is usually good practice to create a dedicated user and group f\
-uu-:**-F1  httpd.conf       29% L109   (Conf[Space])------------------
```

The `Include` directive will tell httpd to load the files with suffix `.conf` in `conf.d` during startup. As we have put `httpd-jk.conf` into `conf.d`, it will be loaded during the httpd startup. Now let's move to JK configuration.

Configuring httpd-jk.conf

We need to configure the JK properly. Please open the `httpd-jk.conf` in `conf.d` and let's check some important configurations:

```
LoadModule jk_module modules/mod_jk.so
```

As shown in the previous code line, we can see that the `mod_jk.so` library is loaded.

```
JkWorkersFile conf/workers.properties
```

By default, JK will find `workers.properties` in the `conf` directory. This property file is used to define our cluster structure. Let's copy the sample `config` file named `workers.properties.minimal` from the JK source directory to `conf.d`:

```
$ cp /packt/tomcat-connectors-1.2.37-src/conf/workers.properties.
  minimal /packt/httpd/conf/workers.properties
```

Later, we'll go through the details in this file. Now, let's go back to check `httpd-jk.conf`:

```
JkLogFile logs/mod_jk.log
```

The `JkLogFile` directive defines the logfile used by JK.

```
JkLogLevel info
```

The `JkLogLevel` directive defines the log level of JK. You can change it to `debug` to see more details when JK is running.

```
JkShmFile logs/mod_jk.shm
```

This is the JK shared memory file. Just keep it as it is. Now, let's see the following two JK modules:

```
<Location /jk-status>
    JkMount jk-status
    Order deny,allow
    Deny from all
    Allow from 127.0.0.1
</Location>
<Location /jk-manager>
    JkMount jk-manager
    Order deny,allow
    Deny from all
    Allow from 127.0.0.1
</Location>
```

The previously mentioned two locations are for JK management components. We can define them in `workers.properties`:

```
worker.list=jk-status
worker.jk-status.type=status
worker.jk-status.read_only=true

worker.list=jk-manager
worker.jk-manager.type=status
```

We can see that `jk-status` and `jk-manager` are actually the same thing:

```
worker.jk-status.type=status
```

Just one of them is `read_only`:

```
worker.jk-status.read_only=true
```

The other one can accept the management command. In this book, we'll just configure JK using the configuration file and won't cover the topic of jk-manager usages. Now, let's go back to the configuration file. The access scope of jk-status and jk-manager are defined in the Location settings:

```
Allow from 127.0.0.1
```

That means we can only access /jk-status and /jk-manager from the localhost. This is secure because we don't want these management components to be accessed remotely. To support it, we need to add a line in conf/httpd.conf. Under the existing Listen section, add another directive:

```
Listen 127.0.0.1:80
```

It should look like the following:

```
● ○ ○                    4. ssh
# ports, instead of the default. See also the <VirtualHost>
# directive.
#
# Change this to Listen on specific IP addresses as shown below to
# prevent Apache from glomming onto all bound IP addresses.
#
#Listen 12.34.56.78:80
Listen 172.16.123.1:80
Listen 127.0.0.1:80

#
# Dynamic Shared Object (DSO) Support
#
# To be able to use the functionality of a module which was built as\
 a DSO you
# have to place corresponding `LoadModule' lines at this location so\
-uu-:---F1  httpd.conf    10% L34    (Conf[Space])-----------------
```

This will let httpd to accept connection from the localhost. That's all we need to do to enable management consoles. Now, let's check workers.properties.

The workers.properties configuration

We will define our cluster structure in workers.properties that we've copied to the conf directory. The content of this file is straightforward, which is shown as follows:

```
worker.list=lb,jk-status

worker.node1.type=ajp13
worker.node1.host=localhost
worker.node1.port=8009

worker.lb.type=lb
```

```
worker.lb.balance_workers=node1

worker.jk-status.type=status
```

The first line of configuration defines two workers: lb and jk-status. We know that jk-status is used for mounting the management component of JK, and its type is status.

For the worker lb, we see that its type is lb:

```
worker.lb.type=lb
```

The lb type defines a load balancer in JK, and it can be used to dispatch user requests to worker nodes. We see that the example provided by JK has one worker node called node1:

```
worker.lb.balance_workers=node1
```

By default, node1 is a node that supports the AJP13 protocol:

```
worker.node1.type=ajp13
worker.node1.host=localhost
worker.node1.port=8009
```

The preceding configuration needs to be modified. We have two worker nodes, which are the two EAP6 servers running on master and slave, and their IP addresses are 10.0.1.13 and 10.0.1.19 as we know.

We know the two EAP6 servers are running in the domain mode and we are using other-server-group, and master is running as the domain controller. So let's check domain.xml on master:

```
<server-group name="other-server-group" profile="full-ha">
    <socket-binding-group ref="full-ha-sockets"/>
</server-group>
<socket-binding-group name="full-ha-sockets" default-
interface="public">
    <socket-binding name="ajp" port="8009"/>
    . . .
</socket-binding-group>
```

The other-server-group uses the full-ha-sockets binding group. And the AJP port is bound to 8009. But don't forget the port-offset settings in host.xml on master and slave. On the master system, we have the following code snippet:

```
<server name="master-server" group="other-server-group" auto-
start="true">
    <socket-bindings port-offset="250"/>
</server>
```

On the slave system, we have the following code snippet:

```
<server name="slave-server" group="other-server-group" auto-
start="true">
    <socket-bindings port-offset="250"/>
</server>
```

So their bound AJP ports are *8009 + 250 = 8259*. According to the settings in these two worker nodes, let's modify the configuration in `workers.properties`. The following comprises the full contents:

```
worker.list=lb,jk-status

worker.master.type=ajp13
worker.master.host=10.0.1.13
worker.master.port=8259

worker.slave.type=ajp13
worker.slave.host=10.0.1.19
worker.slave.port=8259

worker.lb.type=lb
worker.lb.balance_workers=master,slave

worker.jk-status.type=status
```

In the previous configuration file, we configured our two EAP6 servers as the worker nodes of `lb`. The following diagram shows their relationship:

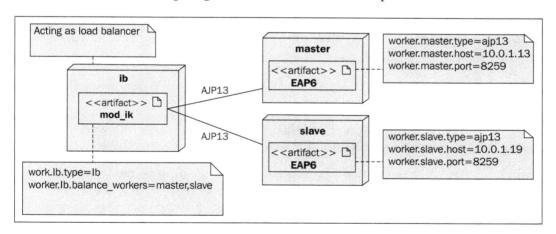

After configuring `workers.properties`, we need to go back to `conf.d/httpd-jk.conf` to add a mount point to our cluster. Under the `JkWorkersFile` directive, add the following line of code:

```
JkMount /* lb
```

The configuration is shown as follows:

```
● ○ ○                         4. ssh
<IfModule jk_module>

    # We need a workers file exactly once
    # and in the global server
    JkWorkersFile conf/workers.properties

    JkMount /* lb□

    # Our JK error log
    # You can (and should) use rotatelogs here
    JkLogFile logs/mod_jk.log

    # Our JK log level (trace,debug,info,warn,error)
    JkLogLevel debug

    # Our JK shared memory file
-uu-:---F1  httpd-jk.conf   21% L31    (Conf[Space])-------------------
```

It will tell httpd to redirect all the HTTP requests to `lb`, and `lb` will proxy the request to EAP6 servers with the AJP13 protocol. That's all for the configuration. Now let's test our cluster.

Testing the cluster

Please shut down the httpd server and then restart it. If you have followed all the instructions in the previous sections, the server should start correctly.

Make sure that you have started two EAP6 servers in the domain mode, and the project `cluster-demo1` has been deployed to `other-server-group`. We'll use these two worker nodes for testing.

As we have bound the public IP address of the load balancer to the hostname `lb`, let's access it by the hostname. Open a web browser and enter the URL `http://lb`.

If everything goes well, we should see the EAP home page now:

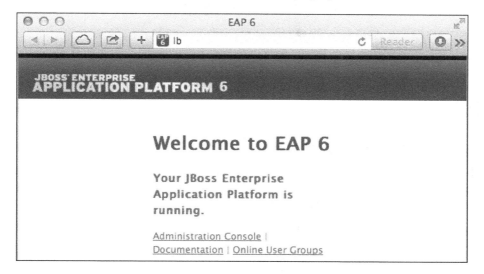

From the previous screenshot, we see that the request is forwarded to the EAP6 servers. Now let's try to access `cluster-demo1`:

```
$ curl http://lb/cluster-demo1/index.jsp
<html>
  <body>
    <h2>Hello World!</h2>

    Hello! The time is now Fri Oct 04 00:31:54 CST 2013
  </body>
</html>
```

We can check the server output of the two EAP6 servers to see which is actually processing this request. In my cluster, this request is handled by `master-server`:

```
[Server:master-server] 00:31:54,264 INFO  [stdout] (ajp-
/10.0.1.13:8259-3) Hello! The time is now Fri Oct 04 00:31:54
CST 2013
```

Let's shut down the EAP6 server that is serving this request. For my cluster, I press *Ctrl + C* on my `master-server` to shut down:

```
00:36:32,078 INFO  [org.jboss.as.process] (Shutdown thread)
  JBAS012015: All processes finished; exiting
```

Then, I use cURL to access the load balancer again. The request is forwarded to another EAP server. It is slave-server processing the user request this time:

```
[Server:slave-server] 00:36:39,966 INFO   [stdout] (ajp-
    /10.0.1.19:8259-4) Hello! The time is now Fri Oct 04 00:36:39 CST
    2013
```

From the users' perspective, they are not affected by one worker node shutdown in the cluster.

The jk-status module

Finally, let's have a brief look at the jk-status module. Open your web browser from the machine of your load balancer. Then, access the jk-status by its URL: http://localhost/jk-status.

We will see the status of two worker nodes:

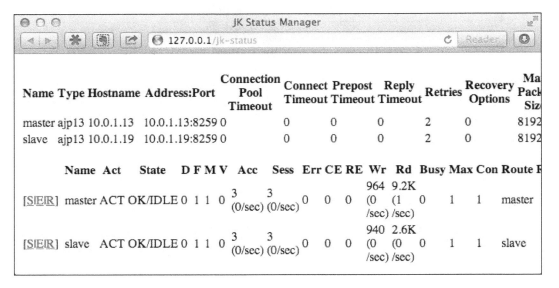

From the previous screenshot, we can check the running statuses of the two EAP6 servers and how many requests they have processed.

Summary

In this chapter, we have learned how to use JK as a load balancer to proxy user requests. As you can see, JK is very easy to use and yet powerful. It relies on `workers.properties` to define the structure of the cluster. When a worker node in a cluster crashes, JK will failover the user requests to other nodes in the cluster. We haven't touched all the features that JK has provided to us, for example, a fine-grained route matching and the usage of `jk-status` for management tasks. You can refer to the JK online document for these topics.

5
Load Balancing with mod_cluster

In this chapter, we will have a look at another load balancer solution. It is called **mod_cluster** (`http://www.jboss.org/mod_cluster`).

In comparison with JK, mod_cluster is more powerful and complex in design. Nevertheless, the added complexity in design doesn't mean it's harder to use; mod_cluster is designed to be scalable and can dynamically find the worker nodes so as to form a cluster.

Such kinds of flexibilities usually create confusion among newcomers and give them the impression that mod_cluster is harder to use. Thus, to appreciate the power of mod_cluster and its simplicity of usage, we must understand its design first.

The design of mod_cluster

From the previous chapter, we know that JK uses a TCP port to communicate with the JBoss EAP6 server via AJP13 protocols. When compared with JK, mod_cluster uses the following three channels to serve its functions:

- A **connector channel** supports the multiple protocols for the load balancer to proxy user requests to worker nodes. This part is almost synonymous with JK. The difference here is that besides the AJP13 protocol, mod_cluster also supports the HTTP/HTTPS protocols.

- An **advertising channel** discovers worker nodes. This channel uses IP multicasting to transfer UDP datagrams. The load balancer will advertise itself in a multicast group, and the worker nodes will find it automatically by subscribing to this group.

- A **management channel** is used to transfer status and management messages between the load balancer and the worker nodes. The protocol used by the management channel is an extension of the HTTP/1.1 protocol. The name of the protocol is **MCMP**.

When compared with JK, mod_cluster can collect many runtime factors of a worker node to judge its "busy-ness", and it calculates a number that indicates the "busy-ness" of each worker node. This number is called a **load factor**, and the factors are called **metrics**.

 mod_cluster provides us with multiple metrics to use, such as `SystemMemoryUsageLoadMetric` and `AverageSystemLoadMetric`. A complete list of metrics can be found here: `http://docs.jboss.org/mod_cluster/1.2.0/html/java.load.html`.

The deployment of mod_cluster is divided into two parts: the first part is the load balancer, and the other part is the worker node. In our scenario, the load balancer is **httpd**, and mod_cluster provides a native component for it. On the worker node side, we are using JBoss EAP6, and mod_cluster provides a subsystem for it. To sum up, let's have an overview of its structure:

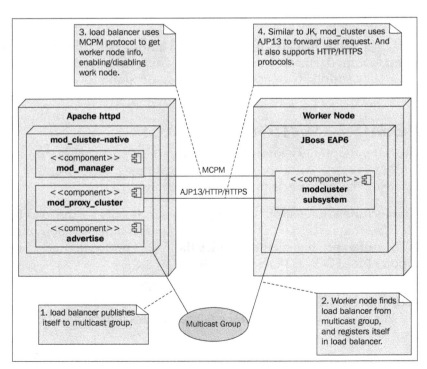

As per the preceding diagram, mod_cluster is divided into two parts: the load balancer side and the worker node side. In addition, it has the following three channels that form its functions:

- The **advertise** channel allows the load balancer to advertise itself, and the worker nodes can dynamically join or exit a cluster at runtime.

- With the **mod_manager** channel, the load balancer can get the load factor information from the worker node. The MCPM protocol is used in this channel, and the load factor, along with the rest of the information of the worker nodes, is sent at regular intervals.

- The **mod_proxy_cluster** channel will forward user requests to the worker nodes from behind. It supports the AJP13 protocol similar to JK, and it supports HTTP/HTTPS additionally.

After this overview of the design of mod_cluster, we will learn how to install mod_cluster in the following section.

Installing mod_cluster

In this section, we will learn how to compile mod_cluster from the source code and install it on our load balancer machine. The machine I'm using to install mod_cluster and httpd is called *lb*, which is the same machine used in the previous chapter.

We have learned how to compile and install httpd in the previous chapter, and we have put a lot of JK-related configurations in our httpd installation. To make the instructions in this chapter clearer, let's archive the following httpd installation from the previous chapter:

```
$ mv httpd httpd-for-jk
```

We'll need to use it in the next chapter, so please back it up properly. Our next step is to repeat the httpd compiling and installing processes as we have done in the previous chapter. We actually just need to rerun `make install` in the httpd source directory because we have already configured and compiled it properly, and we will get a fresh httpd installation by running this command. Now let's move on with the mod_cluster installation.

Downloading mod_cluster

Now we need to download mod_cluster. The source code of mod_cluster is hosted at GitHub. We will use Version 1.2.6.Final in this book: `https://github.com/modcluster/mod_cluster/archive/1.2.6.Final.zip`.

Download it and extract the ZIP file, and you will get the source directory
`mod_cluster-1.2.6.Final`. The following are its contents:

```
⬤ ◯ ◯                                    1. bash
$ ls
JBossORG-EULA.txt         docs                      sar
README.txt                lgpl.txt                  site-mod_cluster
build-test.xml            local.properties          src
container                 mod_cluster-parent.iml test
container-spi             native                    test-jars.xml
core                      pom.xml
demo                      release.txt
$
```

In the source directory, we can see that mod_cluster contains several components,
but we only need to care about the components in the `native` directory. The other
Java modules are for the worker node. Since EAP6 already contains the mod_cluster
subsystem out of the box, we don't need to compile them. Now let's have a look at
the `native` directory:

```
⬤ ◯ ◯                                    1. bash
$ ls
advertise              mod_proxy_cluster selinux
include                mod_slotmem
mod_manager            scripts
$
```

You may have guessed the purposes of some components by their names; let's still
check them one by one:

advertise	The advertising module for the supporting autodiscovery worker node
mod_proxy_cluster	The proxy module that supports the AJP/HTTP/HTTPS proxy requests.
mod_manager	The mod_cluster manager module that controls the worker node and gets load factors from the worker node.
mod_slotmem	The shared memory module used by mod_cluster internally.
selinux	The SElinux policy files. We won't cover this topic in the book.
include	Common header files.
scripts	Some installation scripts we won't use.

As we have understood the meaning of these components, it's now time to build them.

Compiling and installing mod_cluster

The modules that we need to build are advertise, mod_proxy_cluster, mod_manager, and mod_slotmem. It doesn't matter which module you build first; let's start with advertise. We need to find a script called `buildconf` in the directory as follows:

```
mod_cluster-1.2.6.Final/native/advertise$ ls buildconf
buildconf
```

Now let's run this script:

```
$ ./buildconf
```

It will create a script called `configure`. Then we need to run the this script using the following command:

```
$ ./configure  --with-apxs=/packt/httpd/bin/apxs
```

We've used the `--with-apxs` option to tell mod_cluster the position of httpd. After the configuring process is complete, please run the `make` command, and we will get the following shared library named `mod_advertise.so`:

```
● ○ ○                                    2. ssh
-bash-4.2$ ./buildconf
Creating configure ...
-bash-4.2$ ./configure --with-apxs=/packt/httpd/bin/apxs
checking for Apache httpd installation... APXS is /packt/httpd/bin/apxs
apxs_support is true
configure: creating ./config.status
config.status: creating Makefile
-bash-4.2$ make
/usr/lib/apr-1/build/libtool --silent --mode=link gcc -pthread          -o mod_a
dvertise.la -rpath /packt/httpd/modules -module -avoid-version  mod_advertise.lo
/packt/httpd/build/instdso.sh SH_LIBTOOL='/usr/lib/apr-1/build/libtool --silent'
 mod_advertise.la `pwd`
/usr/lib/apr-1/build/libtool --silent --mode=install cp mod_advertise.la /packt/
mod_cluster-1.2.6.Final/native/advertise/
libtool: install: warning: remember to run `libtool --finish /packt/httpd/module
s'
-bash-4.2$ ls *.so
mod_advertise.so
-bash-4.2$ []
```

After the preceding library is built, let's move it to the httpd `modules` folder:

```
$ mv mod_advertise.so /packt/httpd/modules/
```

This is all that we need to do for compiling and installing `advertise`. Go to the directories of the other three modules, and use the same procedure to build them one by one. We'll get `mod_proxy_cluster.so`, `mod_manager.so`, and `mod_slotmem.so`. Please move all of them to the httpd `modules` directory.

These are all the mod_cluster components we need to install. In the following section, we will configure httpd to use these modules.

Configuring mod_cluster

After installing the necessary mod_cluster components in httpd, we will configure them properly in this section.

Configuring httpd.conf

Before we start to configure mod_cluster, we need to do some preparations in `httpd.conf`. The first thing to do is to change the `Listen` directive from `Listen 80` to the following:

```
Listen 10.0.1.33:80
Listen 10.0.1.33:6666
Listen 172.16.123.1:80
```

As we know, *lb* has two IP addresses: one is the public address 172.16.123.1, and the other is 10.0.1.33, which is the internal IP address of the load balancer used to communicate with the two EAP6 servers. Now let's learn the purpose of the configuration:

- `10.0.1.33:80` will be used for a mod_cluster management console. We don't want public access of this management console, so we just bind it to the local IP address.

- `10.0.1.33:6666` will be used by mod_manager to communicate with the EAP6 servers, and the message encapsulated in the MCPM protocol will be transferred through this channel.

- `172.16.123.1:80` is the public address that serves user requests. If you don't have a separate public IP address, you can just use your local IP address to serve all the requests.

After configuring the listening addresses, the next step is to configure the `LogLevel`. We need to change the log level to `debug`; the following is the configuration for doing so:

```
LogLevel debug
```

We need the debug log output later. We will now go to the `ServerName` section and add the hostname of our load balancer. We are using `lb` as the hostname, so the configuration is as shown:

```
ServerName lb
```

And please don't forget to bind this server name to the public IP address in `/etc/hosts`. Next, we need to add an `Include` directive at the bottom of `httpd.conf`:

```
Include conf.d/*.conf
```

This is all we need to do in `httpd.conf`. In the next section, we'll create a separate configuration file for mod_cluster in the `conf.d` directory

Configuring mod_cluster

Now let's create a directory named `conf.d` in httpd:

```
/packt/httpd$ mkdir conf.d
```

Then we need to create a file called `mod-cluster.conf` in the same directory:

```
/packt/httpd/conf.d$ touch mod-cluster.conf
```

Due to the `Include conf.d/*.conf` directive in `httpd.conf`, the created configuration file will be loaded during httpd startup.

Now let's add the contents to this file. First, we need to load the following modules of mod_cluster:

```
LoadModule slotmem_module modules/mod_slotmem.so

LoadModule manager_module modules/mod_manager.so

LoadModule proxy_cluster_module modules/mod_proxy_cluster.so

LoadModule advertise_module modules/mod_advertise.so
```

Note that mod_cluster relies on some of the already configured modules in `httpd.conf`:

```
LoadModule proxy_module modules/mod_proxy.so

LoadModule proxy_ajp_module modules/mod_proxy_ajp.so

LoadModule proxy_http_module modules/mod_proxy_http.so

LoadModule ssl_module modules/mod_ssl.so
```

The preceding modules have already been loaded in `httpd.conf`. Please note that the `proxy-balancer` module is disabled in httpd because it conflicts with mod_cluster.

Now we need to define two virtual hosts: one is for the web management console, and the other is for the management module to send/receive MCPM messages. Let's go through them one at a time. Here's the configuration for the first one:

```
<VirtualHost 10.0.1.32:80>
  <Directory />
    Order deny,allow
    Deny from all
    Allow from 10.0.1
  </Directory>
  <Location /mc>
    SetHandler mod_cluster-manager
    Order deny,allow
    Deny from all
    Allow from 10.0.1
  </Location>
</VirtualHost>
```

In the previous virtual host definition, we have defined a location called `/mc` and bound it to `mod_cluster-manager`. This handler will provide us with a web-based management console, which we'll use in the later sections. Now let's check the second virtual host definition:

```
<VirtualHost 10.0.1.32:6666>
  <Directory />
    Order deny,allow
    Deny from all
    Allow from 10.0.1
  </Directory>
  ServerAdvertise on http://10.0.1.32:6666
  EnableMCPMReceive
</VirtualHost>
```

There are two important directives in the preceding settings. One is the `ServerAdvertise` directive. The address set in this directive will be advertised by mod_cluster in the multicast group. For example, our setting is as follows:

```
ServerAdvertise on http://10.0.1.32:6666
```

So, mod_cluster will broadcast it in a multicast group by saying something to this effect: "My MCPM management channel is located at http://10.0.1.32:6666, come and join me!". The worker nodes that are subscribed to the multicast group will receive this information and can then join the cluster.

Please note that we don't need to configure the multicast address for advertising. This is because the default address for advertising is 224.0.1.105:23364, which matches the default settings in EAP6. We'll see this in the next section. If you want to change this setting, you can use the `AdvertiseGroup` directive by placing it under the `ServerAdvertise` directive:

```
AdvertiseGroup <some_other_multicast_addr:some_other_port>
```

 You can always check the online document for mod_cluster to learn about these detail configurations: (http://docs.jboss.org/mod_cluster/1.2.0/html/native.config.html).

Now let's see the following directive:

```
EnableMCPMReceive
```

With the preceding directive, the virtual host 10.0.1.32:6666 is used as a management channel, and MCPM is used as the communication protocol for this channel. This is all we need to do in `mod-cluster.conf`.

Configuring EAP6

Until now, we haven't looked at the `modcluster` subsystem configuration in EAP6. Since the default configuration provided by the EAP6 domain mode is good to use, we don't need to change anything. Let's have a look at the configuration anyway.

From the configuration in `domain.xml`, we can see the following default settings of the `modcluster` subsystem:

```
<subsystem xmlns="urn:jboss:domain:modcluster:1.1">
    <mod-cluster-config advertise-socket="modcluster" connector="ajp">
        <dynamic-load-provider>
            <load-metric type="busyness"/>
        </dynamic-load-provider>
    </mod-cluster-config>
</subsystem>
```

We can see that the modcluster subsystem is bound to the advertising socket named modcluster by the advertising-socket directive. Then we see that the modcluster subsystem is using the busyness metric by default. It is a metric that judges the server "busy-ness" from the working threads. Now let's see the settings of the socket-binding modcluster:

```
<socket-binding-group name="full-ha-sockets" default-
interface="public">
  <socket-binding name="modcluster" port="0" multicast-
address="224.0.1.105" multicast-port="23364"/>
</socket-binding-group>
```

From the preceding configuration, we can see that 224.0.1.1.105:23364 is the default multicast group address for advertising. This matches the settings on the httpd side.

These settings are of the modcluster subsystem in EAP6. As we have gone through the settings of mod_cluster from both sides, in the following section we will test the cluster.

Testing the cluster

In this section we'll test our cluster, so we need to start our load balancer and EAP6 servers. Before we start httpd on lb, we need to start the two EAP6 servers. After the two EAP6 servers have been started, start httpd. In the following section, we'll examine the process of starting up httpd.

Starting up httpd

Now we need to start the httpd server. If everything goes fine, mod_cluster in httpd will begin to advertise itself in a multicast group, and the modcluster subsystem in the two EAP6 servers will be able to find mod_cluster in httpd by fetching its address in the advertising channel. We will investigate this process in the following sections; let's first start httpd. The command to start httpd on lb is as follows:

```
/packt/httpd/bin$ sudo ./httpd -f /packt/httpd/conf/httpd.conf -k start
```

After httpd has been started, mod_cluster will advertise itself to the multicast group 224.0.1.105:23364, and the modcluster subsystem on the two EAP6 servers will fetch the address of the management channel from the group, which is 10.0.1.32:6666. Then the load balancers and the two EAP6 worker nodes will form a cluster by communicating in the management channel with the MCPM protocol. This process is shown in the following diagram:

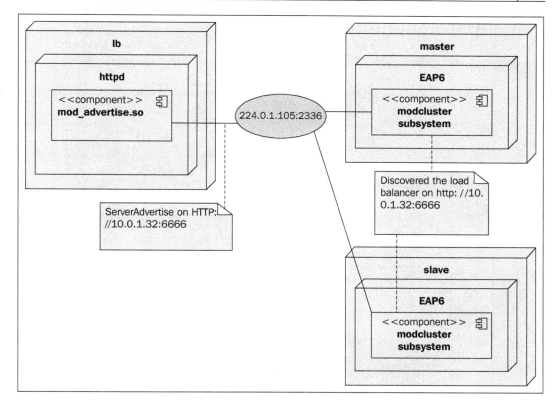

To understand these steps, we need to analyze the packets sent across the network.

The protocol analysis

We can use Wireshark to capture the IP datagrams from one of the worker nodes. In my example I'll run Wireshark on `master`. We can verify the advertising message sent by the load balancer on this machine.

> There is also a small Java program that allows us to join the multicast group and receive the httpd advertisement. See this program at `https://github.com/mod_cluster/mod_cluster/blob/master/test/java/Advertize.java`.

The advertising channel

I have started Wireshark on `master` to capture the IP datagrams. I set it to catch all the datagrams on 224.0.1.105:23364, and the following are my findings:

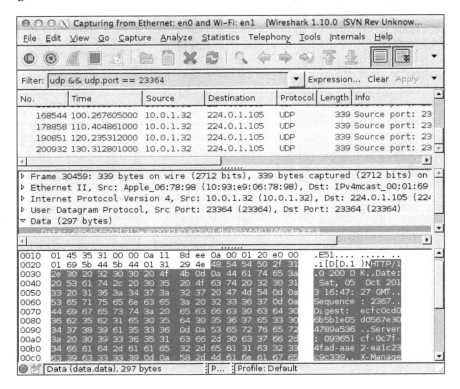

From the preceding screenshot, we can see that `master` is receiving the advertising messages periodically. From the **Time** column, we can see that the advertising message is sent at 10-second intervals.

 You can change this by placing the `AdvertiseFrequency` directive into `conf.d/mod-cluster.conf`.

We can see that the advertising message is in HTTP format. The following are the details of the message:

```
HTTP/1.0 200 OK

Date: Sat, 05 Oct 2013 16:50:49 GMT

Sequence: 2387
```

```
Server: 093651cf-0c7f-4fad-aae2-ea1c23c9c339

X-Manager-Address: 10.0.1.32:6666

X-Manager-Url: /093651cf-0c7f-4fad-aae2-ea1c23c9c339

X-Manager-Protocol: http

X-Manager-Host: cute
```

As shown in the previous code, the advertising message places the load balancer information in the HTTP headers. Among these headers, we should note the value of `X-Manager-Address`. It tells the worker nodes where to find the load balancer. The other headers provide additional information to the worker nodes; this information describes the load balancer.

The management channel

After the worker node comes to know the management address of the load balancer, it will communicate with the load balancer and register itself on it. To see this process, we need to look into the httpd log. As we have set the `LogLevel` to `debug` in `httpd.conf`, we can get many useful details. mod_cluster has outputted a lot of useful log information in the debug level, so we can check `logs/error_log` to see the sequence clearly. Here is the log:

```
[Sat Oct 05 18:09:15 2013] [debug] mod_manager.c(1910): manager_trans
INFO (/)
[Sat Oct 05 18:09:15 2013] [debug] mod_manager.c(2618): manager_handler
INFO (/) processing: ""
[Sat Oct 05 18:09:15 2013] [debug] mod_manager.c(2667): manager_handler
INFO  OK
```

`INFO` is the first MCMP command we've seen till now. This is the command that the worker node uses to request more details of the load balancer. As mod_cluster forms the cluster dynamically, it doesn't know the details of the cluster in advance. The load balancer and worker node just discover each other in the multicast channel, so the worker node needs to know more detailed information about the load balancer. That's why the worker node will send the `INFO` request to the load balancer, and the load balancer will reply with an `INFO-RSP` response.

Now let's see the next step:

```
[Sat Oct 05 18:09:15 2013] [debug] mod_manager.c(1910): manager_trans
CONFIG (/)
[Sat Oct 05 18:09:15 2013] [debug] mod_manager.c(2618): manager_handler
CONFIG (/) processing: "JVMRoute=14a0af8b-59dd-33f9-8233-1f2584fefa67&H
ost=10.0.1.19&Maxattempts=1&Port=8259&StickySessionForce=No&Type=ajp&pi
ng=10"
[Sat Oct 05 18:09:15 2013] [debug] mod_manager.c(2667): manager_handler
CONFIG  OK
```

After the worker node gets the details of the load balancer, it will send to the load balancer a CONFIG message that tells the load balancer the previous worker node details. The JVMRoute is the worker node's name; this is automatically generated by the mod_cluster subsystem in EAP6. Now we know the server 14a0af8b-59dd-33f9-8233-1f2584fefa67 corresponds to the server 10.0.1.19, which is our slave EAP6 server.

Let's check the next step:

```
[Sat Oct 05 18:09:15 2013]  [debug] mod_manager.c(1910):  manager_trans
ENABLE-APP (/)

[Sat Oct 05 18:09:15 2013]  [debug] mod_manager.c(2618):  manager_
handler ENABLE-APP (/) processing: "JVMRoute=14a0af8b-59dd-
33f9-8233-1f2584fefa67&Alias=default-host%2Clocalhost%2Cexample.
com&Context=%2Fcluster-demo1"

[Sat Oct 05 18:09:15 2013]  [debug] mod_manager.c(2667):  manager_handler
ENABLE-APP  OK
```

The worker node sends ENABLE-APP to the load balancer. This is used by the worker node to ask the load balancer to route the request corresponding to the context and the Alias value to the node defined by JVMRoute. In addition, we see the enabled application is cluster-demo1. So if we access the load balancer URL with the route / cluster-demo1, the request will be forwarded to the EAP6 servers. Now let's see the next step:

```
[Sat Oct 05 18:09:15 2013]  [debug] mod_manager.c(1910):  manager_trans
STATUS (/)

[Sat Oct 05 18:09:15 2013]  [debug] mod_manager.c(2618):  manager_
handler STATUS (/) processing: "JVMRoute=14a0af8b-59dd-33f9-8233-
1f2584fefa67&Load=100"

[Sat Oct 05 18:09:15 2013]  [debug] mod_manager.c(1625):  Processing STATUS
```

The worker node sends the STATUS message, which contains its current load factor. From line two of the previous log, we can see that the load factor of the slave EAP6 server is 100 (the smaller the factor number, the busier the server is). This message is sent periodically, and the load factor is refreshed to reflect the real-time status of the worker node. So the load balancer could know which server is busier and send this request to the worker nodes that have a lighter load.

With the previous process, the worker node and load balancer have gathered enough information about each other and established communication. Then the mod_proxy_ cluster.so cluster will start to do the real proxy job. In the following section, we will check this part.

The connector channel analysis

In the previous section, we saw how the load balancer advertises itself and how the worker node discovers it and registers itself into the cluster. Now let's go on to check the `error_log` and see what's going on:

```
[Sat Oct 05 18:09:15 2013] [debug] mod_proxy_cluster.c(655): add_
balancer_node: Create balancer balancer://mycluster

[Sat Oct 05 18:09:15 2013] [debug] mod_proxy_cluster.c(426): Created:
worker for ajp://10.0.1.19:8259

[Sat Oct 05 18:09:15 2013] [debug] proxy_util.c(2018): proxy: ajp: has
acquired connection for (10.0.1.19)

[Sat Oct 05 18:09:15 2013] [debug] proxy_util.c(2074): proxy: connecting
ajp://10.0.1.19:8259/ to 10.0.1.19:8259

[Sat Oct 05 18:09:15 2013] [debug] proxy_util.c(2200): proxy: connected /
to 10.0.1.19:8259
```

As per the preceding log, mod_cluster has established a connection with `ajp://10.0.1.19:8259`. This is the AJP connector of the EAP6 server on the slave host. We can see that mod_cluster has set a name for our cluster, which is `mycluster`. We can check the status of this cluster from the management console. Let's access the management console through its URL, `http://10.0.1.32/mc`.

This is shown in the following screenshot:

[99]

From the preceding screenshot, we can see that the two EAP6 servers form a cluster, and they all belong to `mycluster`. If you want to change the name of the balancer name, you can use the `ManagerBalancerName` directive in `mod-cluster.conf` like this:

```
<VirtualHost 10.0.1.32:6666>
    ...
    ServerAdvertise on http://10.0.1.32:6666
    EnableMCPMReceive
    ManagerBalancerName packtlb
</VirtualHost>
```

As per the previous configuration, the balancer name is set to `packtlb`. Now if we save the changes and restart httpd, we can see the balancer name change accordingly:

```
Node 14a0af8b-59dd-33f9-8233-1f2584fefa67 (ajp://10.0.1.19:8259):

Balancer: packtlb, ...


Node da1db862-4021-36f5-b3ad-b71b61b79c3b (ajp://10.0.1.13:8259):

Balancer: packtlb, ...
```

This is useful when there are multiple load balancers running at the same time. With the balancer name, we can easily see which worker node belongs to which load balancer.

Now let's come back to the debug log; here is the last part we need to look at:

```
[Sat Oct 05 18:09:15 2013] [debug] mod_proxy_cluster.c(1366): proxy_
cluster_try_pingpong: connected to backend
[Sat Oct 05 18:09:15 2013] [debug] mod_proxy_cluster.c(1089): ajp_cping_
cpong: Done
[Sat Oct 05 18:09:15 2013] [debug] proxy_util.c(2036): proxy: ajp: has
released connection for (10.0.1.19)
[Sat Oct 05 18:09:15 2013] [debug] mod_manager.c(2667): manager_handler
STATUS OK
```

After the AJP channels are established, mod_cluster from the httpd side will send `ajp_cping_cpong` messages to the EAP6 worker nodes periodically to check whether the nodes are still alive.

As we have done the protocol analysis, in the following section we'll access the cluster to see if it works properly.

Accessing the cluster

We can access the load balancer using its URL:
`http://lb/cluster-demo1/index.jsp`.

By checking the two EAP6 servers output, we can see that the request is dispatched to `master`:

```
[Server:master-server] 02:34:49,395 INFO  [stdout] (ajp-/10.0.1.13:8259-
4) Hello! The time is now Mon Oct 07 02:34:49 CST 2013
```

Now when we check the mod_cluster management console, we can see that the master server has been elected once:

> # Node da1db862-4021-36f5-b3ad-b71b61b79c3b (ajp://10.0.1.13:8259):
>
> Enable Contexts Disable Contexts
> Balancer: packtlb,LBGroup: ,Flushpackets: Off,Flushwait: 10000,Ping: 10000000,Smax: 26,Ttl: 60000000,Status:
> OK,Elected: 1,Read: 105,Transferred: 0,Connected: 0,Load: 100

As we can see from the preceding screenshot, the **Elected** count becomes **1** for the master server.

Failover

Now let's kill the master server by pressing the *Ctrl + C* keys:

```
02:41:36,977 INFO  [org.jboss.as.process] (Shutdown thread) JBAS012015:
All processes finished; exiting
```

From the slave server, we can see that it starts to throw the following exception because it cannot connect to the master server:

```
[Host Controller] 02:41:47,971 DEBUG [org.jboss.as.host.controller]
(domain-connection-threads - 8) failed to reconnect to the remote host-
controller: java.net.ConnectException: JBAS012144: Could not connect to
remote://10.0.1.13:9999. The connection timed out
```

This is expected because we have killed the master server. But it can still function as a server. Now let's access the load balancer again; we can see that the following request is dispatched to the slave server:

```
[Server:slave-server] 02:44:45,285 INFO  [stdout] (ajp-/10.0.1.19:8259-2)
Hello! The time is now Mon Oct 07 02:44:45 CST 2013
```

Now let's access the mod_cluster management console, and we can see that the master server is removed automatically. In addition, the **Elected** count of the slave server becomes **1**:

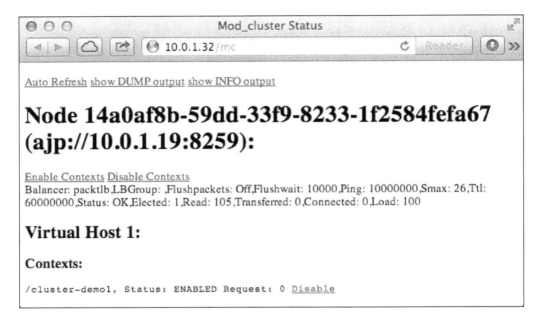

Now let's restart the EAP6 server on the master server, and it will rejoin the cluster. From the httpd debug log output, we can confirm this as follows:

```
[Mon Oct 07 04:01:31 2013] [debug] proxy_util.c(2200): proxy: connected /
to 10.0.1.13:8259
```

From the slave server output, we can see that it also restores the connection to the domain controller:

```
[Host Controller] 04:01:05,379 INFO   [org.jboss.as.host.controller]
(domain-connection-threads - 1) JBAS010916: Reconnected to master
```

Stress testing

Now let's try to use the Apache HTTP server benchmarking tool (called **ab**) to load test our cluster. Here is the command:

```
$ ab -c 15 -n 1500 http://lb/cluster-demo1/index.jsp
```

We've used `15` threads to request our cluster `1500` times. Here are the results:

```
Benchmarking cute (be patient)

Completed 150 requests

...

Finished 1500 requests
```

You can see that ab created some load on mod_cluster. Here are the statuses of the two worker nodes during testing:

Node da1db862-4021-36f5-b3ad-b71b61b79c3b (ajp://10.0.1.13:8259):

Enable Contexts Disable Contexts
Balancer: packtlb,LBGroup: ,Flushpackets: Off,Flushwait: 10000,Ping: 10000000,Smax: 26,Ttl: 60000000,Status: OK,Elected: 1842,Read: 193095,Transferred: 0,Connected: 5,Load: 100

The preceding screenshot depicts the status of the master server, and the status of the slave server is shown in the following screenshot:

Node 14a0af8b-59dd-33f9-8233-1f2584fefa67 (ajp://10.0.1.19:8259):

Enable Contexts Disable Contexts
Balancer: packtlb,LBGroup: ,Flushpackets: Off,Flushwait: 10000,Ping: 10000000,Smax: 26,Ttl: 60000000,Status: OK,Elected: 1929,Read: 202335,Transferred: 0,Connected: 2,Load: 99

We can see that both the worker nodes are elected (the elected counts are more than 1,500 because I've run the preceding tests many times). We can also see that the **Load** factor on slave became **99**. This means the slave server is busier than the master server, so the load balancer will dispatch more requests to the master server later.

Summary

In this chapter, we have looked at the design of mod_cluster and its usages. This chapter is just an introductory text to mod_cluster. If you want to check the more advanced usage, please refer to its constantly improving online document: `http://docs.jboss.org/mod_cluster/1.2.0/html_single/`.

If you have any questions about using mod_cluster, you can always ask questions on the JBoss forum: `https://community.jboss.org/en/mod_cluster/content`.

In the next chapter, we'll see how to apply **Secure Sockets Layer (SSL)** in a clustering environment.

6
Clustering with SSL

In the previous two chapters, we have learnt to use JK and mod_cluster as the load balancer to proxy user requests to EAP6 backend servers, and all the communications between load balancer and EAP6 servers are transferred in *plaintext*. In practice, there are situations where we need to secure the transportation layer by enabling **SSL**. In this chapter, we'll learn how to enable SSL in the clustering environment. We'll first learn how to enable SSL when using JBoss EAP6 independently, and then we'll learn how to enable SSL in a clustering environment that has httpd and EAP6 servers running together. For the clustering environment, we'll use JK as a load balancer in this chapter. Because using mod_cluster has provided a more fine-grained integration with SSL, we'll talk about this topic in the next chapter.

 You need to have some basic knowledge of public key cryptography and SSL before reading this chapter.

Using SSL in JBoss EAP6

First let us see how to enable SSL in EAP6 directly. This is useful when we are using EAP6 as a standalone server and it doesn't have any load balancing in front. JBoss EAP6 provides SSL support out of the box and in this section, let's see how to enable it.

Enabling SSL in EAP6

To enable SSL in EAP6, we need to create an x.509 certificate for the EAP6 server. First prepare a clean copy of JBoss EAP 6.1.0.Final to make sure the configurations are default. After the clean copy of EAP6 server is ready for use, please start it in the standalone mode, and then deploy cluster-demo1 to the running server and then stop the server. That's all we need to do for preparation. We'll use it to test the HTTPS connection later.

Now let's create a directory called certs in the EAP6 base path. We'll use it to store the server certificate.

Then we need to navigate to the certs directory and use the keytool command provided by **Java Runtime Environment (JRE)** to generate a certificate for the EAP6 server. Here is the command:

```
$ keytool -genkey -keystore myserver.ks
```

The running process is shown in the following screenshot:

```
                              2. bash
mini:certs weinanli$ keytool -genkey -keystore myserver.ks
Enter keystore password:
Re-enter new password:
What is your first and last name?
  [Unknown]:  mini
What is the name of your organizational unit?
  [Unknown]:  Personal
What is the name of your organization?
  [Unknown]:  Personal
What is the name of your City or Locality?
  [Unknown]:  Beijing
What is the name of your State or Province?
  [Unknown]:  Beijing
What is the two-letter country code for this unit?
  [Unknown]:  CN
Is CN=mini, OU=Personal, O=Personal, L=Beijing, ST=Beijing, C=CN corr
ect?
  [no]:  yes

Enter key password for <mykey>
        (RETURN if same as keystore password):
mini:certs weinanli$
```

The **keystore password** and **key password** is **packt000**. Please note that in a production environment, we must set **CN** to the hostname of our website. For this example, my hostname is called **mini**, so I use it as **CN** of the certificate. Now let's check the generated `keystore` file and the key that is contained in it:

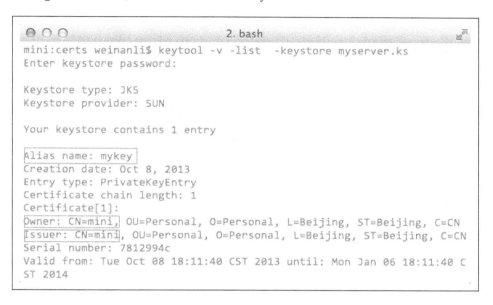

As shown in the preceding screenshot, our generated key and its certificate are stored in `keystore`. The default **Alias name** of the key is **mykey**, and its certificate is associated with it. If we look carefully, we can see that the **Issuer** and the **Owner** of this certificate are the same. That means this is a self-signed certificate. In a production environment, we need to find an authority (like **VeriSign**) to sign this certificate. After the authority has signed it, the **Issuer** will be changed to the authority.

Now we need to configure the EAP6 web subsystem to use the key together with its certificate. Let's open `standalone.xml` and find the subsystem `urn:jboss:domain:web:1.4`. Then we need to find an HTTP connector and change its scheme to HTTPS. Next we need to add an SSL element to tell EAP6 the position of our `keystore` and the alias name of our key. The modifications should be as follows:

```
                <coordinator-environment default-timeout="300"/>
        </subsystem>
        <subsystem xmlns="urn:jboss:domain:web:1.4" default-virtual-\
server="default-host" native="false">
                <connector name="http" protocol="HTTP/1.1" scheme="https\
" socket-binding="https" secure="true">
                        <ssl key-alias="mykey" password="packt000" certifica\
te-key-file="${jboss.home.dir}/certs/myserver.ks" cipher-suite="ALL"\
  protocol="TLS"/>
                </connector>
                <virtual-server name="default-host" enable-welcome-root=\
"true">
-uuu:---F1  standalone.xml   80% L263   (XML)---------------------
```

That's all we need to configure in `standalone.xml`. In addition, please note the port used by HTTPS in the configuration file is `8443`:

```
<socket-binding name="https" port="8443"/>
```

So we need to use this port to access the EAP6 web subsystem. Now we can start the EAP6 server and test the HTTPS connection:

```
$ curl -k https://localhost:8443/cluster-demo1/index.jsp
<html>
<body>
<h2>Hello World!</h2>

Hello! The time is now Tue Nov 19 20:40:52 CST 2013
</body>
</html>
```

The `-k` option of **cURL** is to bypass the certificate verification. Since our certificate is not signed by an authority, by default it's not trusted by cURL or any other web browsers.

In this section, we have learned how to enable SSL in the EAP6 standalone mode. Enabling SSL in the domain mode is similar; we also need to set the web subsystem to use the HTTPS scheme and add the certificate information in the SSL element. I'd like to leave this work to you.

Using SSL in the JBoss EAP6 cluster

In a clustering environment, applying SSL does not seem as straightforward as in a single-server environment. We have a load balancer and worker nodes in a cluster, so we need to decide in which place we should enable SSL. Here are the two possible places:

- The communication between users and the load balancer
- The communication between the load balancer and the worker nodes

In practice, we usually enable SSL between users and the load balancer to secure their communication, and use *cleartext* communication between the load balancer and the worker nodes. Here is the deployment diagram:

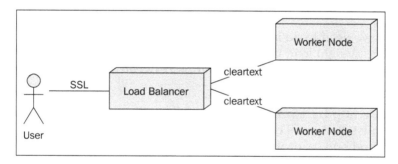

This is reasonable because the worker nodes are usually protected by a firewall, and the purpose of using SSL is not only for encrypting communication channel, but a certificate signed by an authority can also help the customers' web browsers to verify the identity of the web server.

Enabling SSL communication between the load balancer and the worker node also creates many overheads in the communication layer, and encrypting/decrypting network data consumes CPU power.

JK doesn't support the SSL communication between the load balancer and the worker node, and this is not a problem in most situations as I explained earlier, mod_cluster supports the secure connection between the load balancer and the worker node, and we will see how to configure it in the next chapter.

Configuring JK with SSL

Now let's start to learn how to enable SSL with JK. Let's see the deployment diagram first:

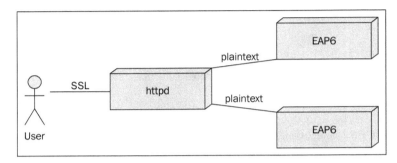

Actually what we need to do is just enable SSL in Apache httpd. As we know, mod_jk is a lightweight load balancer and it only supports the AJP connection to worker nodes. That means the communication between JK and EAP6 servers will be *cleartext* AJP13 protocol.

To enable SSL in httpd, we need to do some preparation work. Please restore httpd with JK installed, we'll configure SSL based on it. If you've forgotten how to configure httpd and JK properly, please read *Chapter 4, Load Balancing with mod_jk* again.

Generating a certificate for httpd

Now let's prepare the server certificate for httpd to use. First, let's create a certs directory in httpd:

```
/packt/httpd$ mkdir certs
```

Then we need to navigate to the `certs` directory and generate a certificate for httpd. For httpd, we'll need to use **OpenSSL** to generate a certificate, because httpd doesn't support the `keystore` format used by Java applications. Actually, the certificate formats are all the same, but the storing structures generated by `keytool` and OpenSSL are different. OpenSSL separates the keys and certificates into standalone files, but `keytool` stores them in a single `keystore` file.

Now let's generate a key, and here is the command and its process:

```
$ openssl genrsa -des3 -out lb.key 1024
Generating RSA private key, 1024 bit long modulus
Enter pass phrase for lb.key: packt000
Verifying - Enter pass phrase for lb.key: packt000
```

Next we need to generate a certificate file relative to this key file. Here is the command and its process:

```
$ openssl req -new -key lb.key -out lb.csr
Enter pass phrase for lb.key: packt000
Country Name (2 letter code) [AU]:CN
State or Province Name (full name) [Some-State]:Beijing
Locality Name (eg, city) []:Beijing
Organization Name (eg, company) [Internet Widgits Pty Ltd]:Personal
Organizational Unit Name (eg, section) []:Personal
Common Name (e.g. server FQDN or YOUR name) []: lb
Email Address []:
A challenge password []:
An optional company name []:
```

Now we get the certificate request file `lb.csr` and its related key file `lb.key`. Next is to sign the certificate request file. Because this certificate is for testing, we don't need to find an authority to sign it. We can use the key file to sign its own certificate request file. So this is a self-signed certificate. Here is the command and the running process:

```
$ openssl x509 -req -days 365 -in lb.csr -signkey lb.key -out
  lb.crt
Signature ok
subject=/C=CN/ST=Beijing/L=Beijing/O=Personal/OU=Personal/CN=kb
Getting Private key
Enter pass phrase for lb.key: packt000
```

The signed certificate file is generated and the name is `lb.crt`. This file is in the standard format, so we can also use `keytool` to check its content, as shown in the following code:

```
$ keytool -v -printcert -file lb.crt
Owner: CN=kb, OU=Personal, O=Personal, L=Beijing, ST=Beijing, C=CN
Issuer: CN=kb, OU=Personal, O=Personal, L=Beijing,
   ST=Beijing, C=CN
```

From the previous code snippet, we can see that the `Owner` and `Issuer` of this certificate are same. That was the process to generate a self-signed certificate with OpenSSL. Actually, we can wrap up the preceding processes into a single command:

```
$ openssl req -new -newkey rsa -days 365 -x509 -subj
   "/C=CN/ST=Beijing/L=Beijing/O=Personal/OU=Personal/CN=httpd" -
   keyout lb.key -out lb.crt
```

Using the preceding command, we can generate a key file and its self-signed certificate in one step.

Configuring httpd to use certificates

We need to add several directives into `httpd.conf`. The first step is to ask httpd to listen to port `443`, this is the standard port of https. I'm reusing the cluster configuration from the previous two chapters, so I'm still running my httpd on the machine `lb`, and I'll configure it to listen to the public SSL port:

```
Listen 172.16.123.1:443
```

And don't forget to comment out the access to port 80, because we don't want users to connect without HTTPS:

```
#Listen 172.16.123.1:80
```

Now we need to configure JK, and its configuration file is in `conf.d/httpd-jk.conf`. Please delete all the contents inside and replace it with the following content:

```
LoadModule jk_module modules/mod_jk.so

<IfModule jk_module>
  JkWorkersFile conf/workers.properties
  JkShmFile logs/mod_jk.shm
  JkWatchdogInterval 60

  <VirtualHost 172.16.123.1:443>
    SSLEngine on
    SSLCertificateFile /packt/httpd/certs/lb.crt
```

```
SSLCertificateKeyFile /packt/httpd/certs/lb.key

    JkMount /* lb
    JkLogFile logs/mod_jk.log
    JkLogLevel debug
  </VirtualHost>
</IfModule>
```

As shown in the preceding configuration, we have added a `VirtualHost` bound to the port `443`. In addition, we have enabled the SSL engine and provided the server certificate and its key files to use. Moreover, we have put the JkMount point inside this virtual host, so the user requests to HTTPS will be proxied by `JK` and sent to the EAP6 servers in behind.

That's all we need to configure in httpd. Because the communication between httpd and the EAP6 servers are still using the plaintext AJP13 protocol, so we don't need to change any configuration in EAP6. Now we can start the EAP6 servers and the httpd server. During the httpd server startup, it needs us to input the pass phrase of our key. The process is shown in the following code snippet:

```
$ sudo httpd -k start -f /packt/httpd/conf/httpd.conf
Apache/2.2.25 mod_ssl/2.2.25 (Pass Phrase Dialog)
```

Some of your private key files are encrypted for security reasons.

In order to read them you have to provide the pass phrases.

```
Server localhost:443 (RSA)
Enter pass phrase: packt000

OK: Pass Phrase Dialog successful.
```

If you have set `LogLevel` to `debug` in `httpd.conf`, you can see many SSL-related log outputs in `logs/error_log`. It's a good source to do analysis if anything goes wrong. Now we can access the load balancer by using HTTPS and see that the requests are forwarded to the EAP6 servers:

```
$ curl -k https://172.16.123.1/cluster-demo1/index.jsp
<html>
<body>
<h2>Hello World!</h2>

Hello! The time is now Tue Nov 19 22:40:52 CST 2013
</body>
</html>
```

If we use **Wireshark** to monitor the proxy channel between httpd and EAP6, we can see they are still using the *plaintext* AJP13 protocol to communicate:

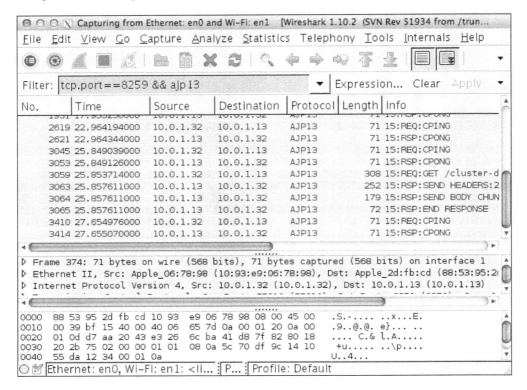

Summary

In this chapter, we have got an overview on applying SSL to EAP6 and the clustering environment, and we have seen how to configure SSL and JK together into httpd. In the next chapter, we'll learn how to apply SSL with mod_cluster.

7
Configuring mod_cluster with SSL

In the previous chapter, we learned how to use SSL with JK (mod_jk). In this chapter, we will check the design of mod_cluster first, and discuss how it can be used with SSL. Then we will learn how to configure the httpd and EAP6 servers so that they can use SSL.

First, let's check the design of mod_cluster.

The design of mod_cluster

As we have seen in the last chapter, JK uses the AJP13 protocol between the load balancer and worker nodes. In comparison to JK, mod_cluster allows us to secure its communication channels.

In design, mod_cluster uses three channels for communication: the advertising channel, the management channel, and the proxy channel. mod_cluster allows us to secure the communication in the management and proxy channels.

The following is the deployment diagram:

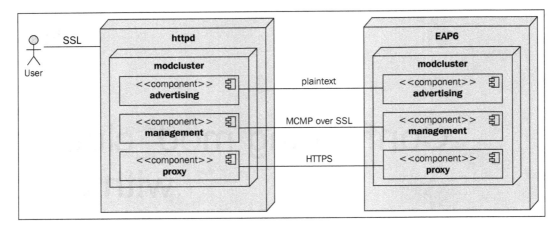

As we can see from the preceding diagram, SSL communications can be enabled in the following three places:

- Communication between users and httpd
- The mod_cluster management channel communication between httpd and EAP6
- The mod_cluster proxy channel communication between httpd and EAP6

We learned how to enable SSL communication between users and httpd in the previous chapter. We need to generate a self-signed certificate and configure mod_ssl in httpd to use the certificate. The following is the configuration that we used in the previous chapter:

```
SSLEngine on
SSLCertificateFile /packt/httpd/certs/lb.crt
SSLCertificateKeyFile /packt/httpd/certs/lb.key
```

The preceding configuration is actually for mod_ssl; so, it remains unchanged when we switch our load balancer component from JK to mod_cluster.

 Please check the `mod-cluster-ssl.conf` file in this chapter's code.

In addition to the pure mod_ssl support of httpd to enable SSL communication between users and httpd, mod_cluster provides additional functions to secure data transmission between the httpd and EAP6 servers. In the following sections, we will have a look at how to enable secure communication for the other two places that are mentioned. First, we'll learn how to enable SSL in the mod_cluster management channel.

Enabling SSL for the mod_cluster management channel

In this section, we will learn how to secure the MCMP channel. This means that the MCMP messages will be transferred over SSL.

 In the mod_cluster documentation, we named the protocol MCMP, which stands for **Mod-Cluster Management Protocol**.

In design, mod_cluster uses SSL mutual authentication to secure the MCMP channel. This means that we must create certificates for both the servers. EAP6 needs to trust the certificate provided by httpd; meanwhile, httpd must trust the certificate from the EAP6 server. So, we need two certificates instead of just one.

An introduction to SSL mutual authentication

In the previous chapter, we created a self-signed certificate for httpd to enable HTTPS communication with users. When users use the web browser to access our website, httpd will provide its certificate to the web browser. If a user chooses to trust the certificate, the web browser will establish a secure connection with our server. This is called one-way authentication. It means that the user will verify the identity of the website, but the website won't verify the identity of the user.

Since our certificate is self-signed, the web browser will pop up a warning to tell the user that it cannot verify the identity of this certificate, and the user will need to decide whether to trust it or not. But if our certificate is signed by an authority, the web browser will trust our certificate without any pop-up warning messages. This is because every web browser contains a default list of authorities. The certificates signed by these authorities will be trusted by default.

For example, I can see the following list of default CAs in my Firefox browser:

Firefox will trust the certificates signed by these authorities only. JDK also contains one such list that is usually the `$JAVA_HOME/jre/lib/security/cacerts` file.

Now, let's talk about encrypting the communication between httpd and EAP6. First, we will learn about one-way authentication. This scenario is shown in the following diagram:

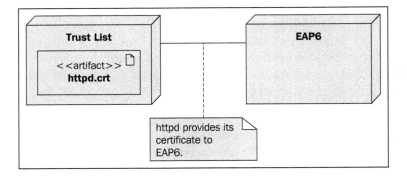

Since EAP6 is running in JVM, it trusts a default list of CAs. Our self-signed certificate is obviously not signed by these authorities; so, by default, EAP6 won't trust it.

To solve this problem, we can create an authority ourselves, and sign the certificate using this authority. Then we can place the authority in EAP6 to override the default trust list so that EAP6 trusts the certificate signed by it. This scenario is shown in the following diagram:

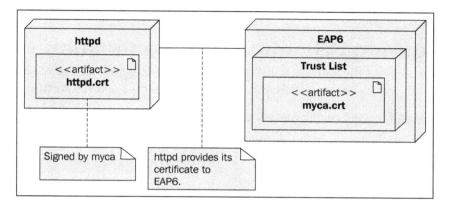

With the previous method, we can establish a one-way authentication from httpd to EAP6. If we want to establish a mutual SSL authentication, we need to additionally create a certificate for EAP6, and sign it with myca. Then, we need to configure httpd to put myca in its trust list so that it trusts the EAP6 certificate. The following diagram shows this scenario:

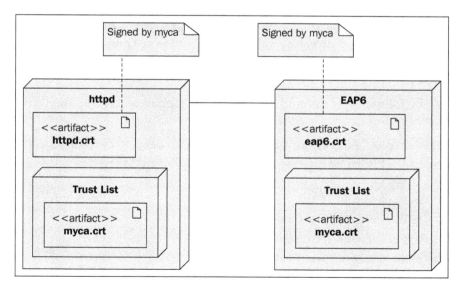

As we can see from this diagram, **httpd** will show its certificate to **EAP6**, and **EAP6** will show its certificate to **httpd.** Only then will they trust each other because their certificates are signed by myca as myca is in their trust list. mod_cluster enforces this mutual SSL authentication. In the following sections, we will learn how to configure httpd and EAP6 properly.

Configuring SSL mutual authentication

As we have learned the concepts of SSL mutual authentication, let's now configure our environment to enable it. We need to create the following three certificates:

- One self-signed certificate as the authority. Let's name it myca.crt.
- One certificate for httpd, signed by myca. Let's name it httpd.crt.
- One certificate for EAP6, signed by myca. Let's name it eap6.crt.

Let's create them one by one.

Creating a CA certificate

First, we will create a CA certificate. The term **CA** stands for **Certificate Authority**; it's actually a self-signed certificate that will be used to sign the other certificates. If one application puts this CA into its trust list, the certificates that are signed by it will be trusted.

We'll create a self-signed certificate named myca and use it as our CA. Before we create it, please prepare a directory called certs and place it appropriately. Since we'll create three certificates along with their key files, it's better to put them together. For me, I'll put it in /packt/certs.

Please use the following command to create a self-signed certificate together with its key file:

```
$ opensslreq -new -newkeyrsa -days 365 -x509 -subj "/C=CN/ST=Beijing/
L=Beijing/O=Personal/CN=myca" -keyoutmyca.key -out myca.crt

Generating a 2048 bit RSA private key

..++++++

.....................++++++

writing new private key to 'myca.key'

Enter PEM pass phrase: packt000

Verifying - Enter PEM pass phrase: packt000

-----
```

With the preceding command, I have generated a key pair with its self-signed certificate, and the CN of this certificate is myca. We can see this by checking the content of the certificate as follows:

```
$ keytool -printcert -file myca.crt | head -n 2
Owner: CN=myca, O=Personal, L=Beijing, ST=Beijing, C=CN
Issuer: CN=myca, O=Personal, L=Beijing, ST=Beijing, C=CN
```

As we can see, the Owner and Issuer are the same. Now, let's create a certificate for httpd, and sign it with myca.

Creating a certificate for httpd

As we have the authority myca now, let's create a certificate for httpd and then sign it with myca. We first need to create a key pair for httpd with the following command:

```
$ openssl genrsa -des3 -out httpd.key 1024
Generating RSA private key, 1024 bit long modulus
.........++++++
.....................................................++++++
e is 65537 (0x10001)
Enter pass phrase for httpd.key: packt000
Verifying - Enter pass phrase for httpd.key: packt000
```

As we can see from the preceding command, the key file is named httpd.key. Next, we'll create a certificate related to the key pair; the following command does this:

```
$ openssl req -new -key httpd.key -out httpd.csr -subj "/C=CN/ST=Beijing/
L=Beijing/O=Personal/CN=httpd"
Enter pass phrase for httpd.key: packt000
```

Please note that the CN value of our certificate is httpd. As a result of running the previous command, we get the http.csr file that waits to be signed. Now, we need to use the tools provided by OpenSSL to sign this certificate with myca, but before that we need to set up OpenSSL properly.

Setting up OpenSSL

OpenSSL has its own workflow for signing the certificate. Please run the following command to set up the working environment for OpenSSL:

```
$ mkdir -p demoCA/newcerts
$ touch ./demoCA/index.txt
$ touch ./demoCA/serial
$ echo "01" > ./demoCA/serial
```

Our signed certificate will be placed in the newcerts directory and named 01.pem. Please make sure that you have run the previous command from the certs directory that contains the myca and httpd certificates.

The next step is to loosen the signing policy in OpenSSL. First, we need to locate the configuration file that OpenSSL is using. Please run the following command:

```
$ openssl ca
Using configuration from /etc/pki/tls/openssl.cnf
...
```

We can see the location of the configuration file used by OpenSSL from the previous command. Let's open openssl.cnf and find the policy_match section. Other than commonName, we need to change all the items in this section to optional. The following screenshot lists the details:

```
# For the CA policy
[ policy_match ]
#countryName            = match
#stateOrProvinceName    = match
#organizationName       = match
countryName             = optional
stateOrProvinceName     = optional
organizationName        = optional
organizationalUnitName  = optional
commonName              = supplied
emailAddress            = optional

-uu-:%%-F1   openssl.cnf   26% L94   (Fundamental)-----------------
```

In addition, we need to change the default directory that OpenSSL will use to sign the certificates; this is done as follows:

```
#dir = /etc/pki/CA
dir = demoCA
```

We are changing the OpenSSL defaults merely for testing purposes. In practice, this will loosen the security of the certificates.

We should always use the default positions for signing certificates and carefully manage their permissions in production environment.

In addition, a real CA faculty will usually require you to provide a certificate with the valid information that it requires. For example, a requirement could be that your certificate's CN must match your DNS hostname, and your country's name must match your host location.

Signing the httpd.csr file

Since we have set OpenSSL properly, we can now start signing our httpd certificate. Please make sure that you are in the `certs` directory, and that it includes a `demoCA` directory with the necessary file contents. Please run the following command to sign the httpd certificate:

```
$ openssl ca -in httpd.csr -keyfile myca.key -cert myca.crt
Using configuration from /etc/pki/tls/openssl.cnf
Enter pass phrase for myca.key: packt000
Check that the request matches the signature
Signature ok
Certificate Details:
...
Sign the certificate? [y/n] :y
1 out of 1 certificate requests certified, commit? [y/n] y
Write out database with 1 new entries
...
Data Base Updated
```

Now, we have signed `httpd.csr`; this signed certificate is located in `demoCA/ newcerts`, and is named `01.pem`. Let's check the content of this certificate:

```
$ cat demoCA/newcerts/01.pem
Certificate:
Issuer: C=CN, ST=Beijing, L=Beijing, O=Personal, CN=myca
Subject: CN=httpd, C=CN, ST=Beijing, O=Personal
```

We can see that the Subject value is httpd and the Issuer value is myca. So we've used our own CA to sign our certificate. Let's copy this certificate into the certs directory and rename it to httpd.crt:

```
$ cpdemoCA/newcerts/01.pem httpd.crt
```

That's all for the httpd certificate. Now, let's work on the EAP6 server, create a certificate for it, and also sign this with myca.

Creating a certificate for EAP6

The processes in the EAP6 server are different; first, we need to use the keytool command to create a keystore with a self-signed certificate. Then, we will export the certificate from the keystore, and sign it with myca. Later, we'll import myca.crt into the keystore to act as a trust authority. So, all the certificates signed by myca will be trusted and accepted by JVM. After that, we'll import the signed EAP6 certificate back to the keystore.

First, let's create a keystore. The keystore file eap6.ks will have the default key pair and a self-signed certificate that is related to the key pair. The following is the command for creating the keystore:

```
$ keytool -genkey -keystoreeap6.ks -storepass packt000 -keypass
packt000 -keyalg RSA -validity 365 -alias eap6cert -dname
"cn=eap6,o=Personal,c=CN,ST=Beijing,L=Beijing"
```

From the preceding command, we can see that the keystore is named eap6.ks, and the alias of the certificate is eap6cert. The cn field of the certificate has a value of eap6, and this certificate is self-signed by default. We can check this with the keytool command:

```
$ keytool -list -v -keystore eap6.ks -storepass packt000 -alias eap6cert
Alias name: eap6cert
...
Owner: CN=eap6, O=Personal, C=CN, ST=Beijing, L=Beijing
Issuer: CN=eap6, O=Personal, C=CN, ST=Beijing, L=Beijing
...
```

Now, let's export eap6cert for the signing request using the following command:

```
$ keytool -certreq -keyalg RSA -alias eap6cert -file eap6cert.csr
-keystoreeap6.ks -storepass packt000
```

With the preceding command, we get the **Certificate Signing Request (CSR)** file, eap6cert.csr. We need to sign this certificate with myca. The process is exactly the same as it was for the signing of the httpd.csr file. We need to place eap6cert.csr in the certs directory, and we need to reuse the demoCA directory that is created for signing the httpd certificate. Please note that we don't need to reset the serial number in ./demoCA/serial, and don't delete the httpd certificate 01.pem from the newcerts directory. OpenSSL will automatically increase the serial number, and the signed EAP6 certificate will be named 02.pem. The following code snippet denotes the signing process:

```
$ opensslca -in eap6cert.csr -keyfilemyca.key -cert myca.crt
Using configuration from /etc/pki/tls/openssl.cnf
Enter pass phrase for myca.key: packt000
Check that the request matches the signature
Signature ok
Certificate Details:
...
Sign the certificate? [y/n]:y
1 out of 1 certificate requests certified, commit? [y/n]y
Write out database with 1 new entries
Certificate:
...
Data Base Updated
```

With this process, the EAP6 certificate is signed and stored in demoCA/serial/02.pem. Now, let's copy 02.pem to eap6raw.crt:

```
$ cp demoCA/newcerts/02.pem eap6raw.crt
```

We can check the contents of this certificate as follows:

```
Issuer: C=CN, ST=Beijing, L=Beijing, O=Personal, CN=myca
Subject: CN=eap6, C=CN, ST=Beijing, O=Personal
```

From the `Issuer` and `Subject` fields, we can see that the certificate is signed. In addition, we can see the encoded certificate data at the bottom of this file. Let's use the following command to extract the encoded certificate text from `eap6raw.crt`:

```
$ grep -A 50 "BEGIN CERTIFICATE" eap6raw.crt
-----BEGIN CERTIFICATE-----
MIIChTCCAe6gAwIBAgIBAjANBgkqhk...
...
bzCk0wKoQRWOZ5lCXUfN9OEOnVbYcBXTAQ==
-----END CERTIFICATE-----:
```

The Java security library can only read the certificate in the previously encoded format, and doesn't allow any extra text in the certificate file. So, we need to extract the encoded certificate data to another file using the following command:

```
$ grep -A 50 "BEGIN CERTIFICATE" eap6raw.crt >eap6cert.crt
```

With the preceding command, we have extracted the encoded certificate data to `eap6cert.crt`; only then can the `keytool` command read it correctly. The following is the command to be used:

```
$ keytool -printcert -file eap6cert.crt   | head -n 2
Owner: O=Personal, ST=Beijing, C=CN, CN=eap6
Issuer: CN=myca, O=Personal, L=Beijing, ST=Beijing, C=CN
```

Now we need to import this signed certificate back to our keystore; the `keytool` command will help us to update the self-signed certificate in the keystore with this signed one. Before doing this, we need to import myca into the keystore. Since our EAP6 certificate is signed by myca and our keystore currently doesn't contain myca, it will reject any certificate that is signed by it. The following command imports myca into the keystore:

```
$ keytool -import -v -trustcacerts -alias myca -file myca.crt
-keystoreeap6.ks -storepass packt000
...
Trust this certificate? [no]:  yes
Certificate was added to keystore
[Storing eap6.ks]
```

Please note the `-trustcacerts` option in the preceding command. We use this option to mark `myca` as a trusted signing authority. Now we can import the `eap6cert.crt` file so that it is accepted by the keystore; we use the following command to do so:

```
$ keytool -import -v -alias eap6cert -file eap6cert.crt -keystoreeap6.ks
-storepass packt000
Certificate reply was installed in keystore
[Storing EAP6.ks]
```

Let's have a look at the certificates in the keystore:

```
$ keytool -list -keystore eap6.ks -storepass packt000
Keystore type: JKS
Keystore provider: SUN


Your keystore contains 2 entries


eap6cert, Dec 2, 2013, PrivateKeyEntry,
Certificate fingerprint (MD5): …
myca, Dec 2, 2013, trustedCertEntry,
Certificate fingerprint (MD5): …
```

From the preceding command output, we can see that there are two entries in the keystore. These two entries have different types: `eap6cert` is a `PrivateKeyEntry`, which means it is a certificate that can be used for identification, and `myca` is a `trustedCertEntry`, which means that it is an authority, and all the other certificates signed by it will be trusted.

We have prepared all the certificates properly. Next, we'll configure httpd and EAP6 so that we can use these certificates properly.

 Please check the code provided with this chapter. In the `certs` directory, you can see all of the sample certificates that we've generated in this section.

Configuring httpd

To enable secure communication in the management channel, we'll need to add several SSL directives to the virtual host that is relative to the surrounding `<VirtualHost>`, as shown in the following configuration:

```
<VirtualHost 10.0.1.32:6666>
SSLEngine on
SSLCertificateFile /packt/httpd/certs/httpd.crt
SSLCertificateKeyFile /packt/httpd/certs/httpd.key
SSLCertificateChainFile /packt/httpd/certs/myca.crt
<Directory />
    Order deny,allow
      Deny from all
      Allow from 10.0.1
</Directory>
ServerAdvertise on https://10.0.1.32:6666
EnableMCPMReceive
ManagerBalancerNamepacktlb
</VirtualHost>
```

The `httpd.crt` file is used by httpd to identify itself, and will be sent to EAP6 for authentication. The `myca.crt` file will be used to authenticate the certificate that EAP6 sends to httpd. As we know, the certificate of EAP6 is signed by `myca`; so, httpd will trust it.

That's all that we need to do for the httpd configuration.

 Please check the `mod-cluster-ssl-mcmp.conf` configuration in this chapter's code.

Now let's configure the EAP6 part.

Configuring EAP6

In EAP6, we need to place our certificate and truststore in the configuration file of the `mod_cluster` subsystem of `domain.xml`. The following are its contents:

```
<subsystem xmlns="urn:jboss:domain:mod_cluster:1.1">
  <mod-cluster-config ...>
        ...
<ssl key-alias="eap6cert" password="packt000" certificate-key-file="/
packt/certs/eap6.ks" ca-certificate-file="/packt/certs/eap6.ks"/>
  </mod-cluster-config>
</subsystem>
```

Since both the server certificate `eap6cert` and the CA certificate `myca` are in the keystore `eap6.ks`, we will use them as `certificate-key-file` and `ca-certificate-file` respectively. EAP6 will show the `eap6cert` certificate to httpd, and it will be trusted by httpd because it's signed by myca.

 Please check the `domain-ssl-mcmp.xml` file in this chapter's code.

At last, we have a very important step left: we need to copy the `eap6.ks` keystore on both the master and slave servers, and place it in the position `/packt/certs/eap6.ks`, just as we've done in the previous code snippet. Since all the worker nodes are using the configuration from `domain.xml`, all the EAP6 servers need this keystore file.

Finally, all the configurations are done. Now let's test the cluster.

Testing the configuration

To test our configuration, let's start httpd and two EAP6 servers. Then we can use cURL to access our cluster:

```
$ curl-k https://172.16.123.1/cluster-demo1/index.jsp
<html>
  <body>
    <h2>Hello World!</h2>

    Hello! The time is now Mon Oct 14 01:52:56 CST 2013
  </body>
</html>
```

The preceding code snippet shows that the load balancer is working. If we use Wireshark to monitor the management channel, we can see the SSL protocol in action:

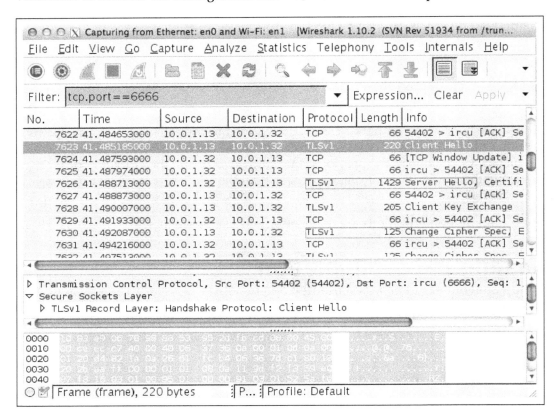

This verifies that the management channel is secured. If we check the data transmission in the proxy channel, we can see that it is still using the plaintext AJP13 protocol:

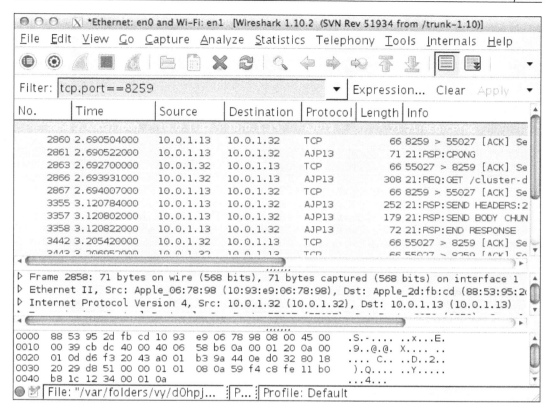

In the following section, we'll see how to enable SSL in the proxy channel.

Enabling SSL in the proxy channel

In this section, we'll configure mod_cluster to use HTTPS instead of AJP13 for the proxy channel.

Since we have prepared the necessary certificates in the previous sections, enabling HTTPS for the proxy channel won't be a difficult task. First, let's check the configuration in the httpd server. We need to add an SSLProxyEngine On configuration to the virtual host to enable public access:

```
<VirtualHost 172.16.123.1:443>
    . . .
SSLProxyEngine On
    . . .
</VirtualHost>
```

As we can see from the preceding configuration, it tells httpd that we need to use an SSL connection for the proxy channel, and that's all that we need to configure httpd.

 The sample configuration file is `mod-cluster-ssl-full.conf`.

Now we need to configure the EAP6 server. In `domain.xml`, we need to change the mod_cluster connector from `ajp` to `https`, as shown in the following code snippet:

```
<subsystem xmlns="urn:jboss:domain:mod_cluster:1.1">
<!--<mod-cluster-config advertise-socket="mod_cluster"
connector="ajp">-->
<mod-cluster-config advertise-socket="mod_cluster" advertise="true"
sticky-session="true" sticky-session-remove="false" sticky-session-
force="false" connector="https">
...
</mod-cluster-config>
</subsystem>
```

Then, we need to turn off the `ajp` connector, and add the `https` connector, as follows:

```
<!--<connector name="ajp" protocol="AJP/1.3" scheme="http" socket-
binding="ajp" enabled="true"/>-->
<connector name="https" protocol="HTTP/1.1" scheme="https" socket-
binding="https" secure="true">
<ssl name="https" key-alias="eap6cert"
    password="packt000"
    certificate-key-file="/packt/certs/eap6.ks"
    protocol="TLS"
verify-client="false"
    certificate-file="/packt/certs/eap6.ks"
ca-certificate-file="/packt/certs/eap6.ks"/>
</connector>
```

Since we are enforcing the SSL connection, we need to turn off the `ajp` connector to prevent the others from using this plaintext communication port.

 The sample configuration file is `domain-ssl-full.xml`.

After restarting the EAP6 server, we can see that the proxy channel starts using HTTPS for communication. The Wireshark analysis is shown in the following screenshot:

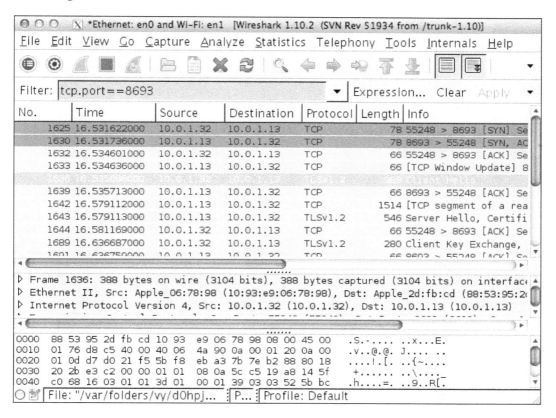

Summary

In this chapter, we learned the different ways to use SSL with mod_cluster. We usually just need to secure the transportation layer for public access, and use plaintext communication between httpd and EAP6 because we protect the worker nodes by placing them in a local network. Please choose a proper solution to meet your requirements. In the next chapter, we will learn how to develop and deploy a distributed project to a cluster.

8
Developing Distributed Applications

In the previous chapters, we have all concentrated on building a stateless cluster. That means we don't need to maintain a session for each user request, and a load balancer can freely choose a worker node to serve the user requests.

A stateless cluster is more flexible and can scale well, so it's always the first choice when we are building a cluster. In essence, HTTP is a stateless protocol, so it lacks the ability to maintain a session for user requests. To solve this problem, web servers usually pass a session ID to the users' web browsers to maintain a long conversation.

For example, if we are building an online shopping system, we have to maintain a shopping cart for each user. When a user is checking out his/her cart, the total price of the goods in the shopping cart will be calculated. All this data needs to be stored either on the server side or in the cookies of users' web browsers and the data needs to be held across multiple pages, so the session ID is the key to refer to this data of a user. For JBoss EAP, the session ID is called JSESSIONID.

In a clustering environment, the situation becomes more complex, because there are multiple servers instead of just one, so their statuses need to be replicated. For example, if a worker node A is serving one user's request, then the data of the shopping cart may be saved on the worker node A. If the load balancer now redirects the user request to the worker node B, then the user will find that his/her shopping cart becomes empty. Even if the JSESSIONID is passed to worker B, the data related with the JSESSIONID is stored in worker A. So the data of the user still gets lost.

There are two ways that are commonly used to solve this problem. The first option is named **sticky sessions**. This is a straightforward way to solve the problem. It means the load balancer will stick a user session to a specific worker node. For example, if one user visits our website and the load balancer chooses worker node A to serve the request, then this worker node will be used forever to serve the following requests from this user until he or she quits the web browser or the session ends.

This solution is easy to apply, and it fits many situations in practice. However, it only partly solves the problem, because a worker node may fail, and the load balancer would like to failover the user requests to another worker node. In this situation, all the sessions on the crashed worker node will still get lost.

So here is the second solution to avoid the preceding problem, it is better for the worker nodes to replicate the session data among one another. Thus when one worker crashes, its session can be restored from other workers.

In this chapter, we will learn how to configure session replications between EAP6 servers, and then we'll see how to configure sticky sessions in httpd.

Web session replication

EAP6 provides web session replication out of the box when it's running in the domain mode (or in the standalone mode with the `*-ha` profile enabled). The session replication is supported by the Infinispan subsystem, and the session container is defined in `domain.xml` (and `standalone-*-ha.xml`):

```
<cache-container name="web" aliases="standard-session-cache"
  default-cache="repl" module=
  "org.jboss.as.clustering.web.infinispan">
  ...
</cache-container>
```

In this section, we'll use a sample project to demonstrate the usage of web session replication. The project is named as `clusterbench`. It has been developed by my colleagues *Radoslav Husar* and *Michal Babacek* at Red Hat.

> The project is located at
> `https://github.com/clusterbench/clusterbench`.

This project has some excellent demonstration codes for us to use. So we'll directly deploy it into our EAP6 servers for testing.

In the demo project, there is a submodule called `clusterbench-ee6-web`. In this module, we can see how the session is enabled in `web.xml`. It uses a single line of configuration to enable web session replication as shown in the following screenshot:

With `distributable` enabled in `web.xml`, the web sessions will be replicated across the EAP6 servers. This is a JavaEE standard requirement. As JBoss EAP6 conforms to the JavaEE standard, it supports this feature. This web project has also provided us a servlet for testing:

```
@WebServlet(name = "HttpSessionServlet", urlPatterns = {"/session"})
public class HttpSessionServlet extends CommonHttpSessionServlet {
}
```

The preceding class `HttpSessionServlet` extends the `CommonHttpSessionServlet`. The `CommonHttpSessionServlet` is defined in `clusterbench-common`. Here is an abstract of the `CommonHttpSessionServlet`:

```
public class CommonHttpSessionServlet extends HttpServlet {

@Override
protected void doGet(HttpServletRequestreq,
HttpServletResponseresp)
throws ServletException, IOException {
HttpSession session = req.getSession(true);
```

```
if (session.isNew()) {
log.log(Level.INFO, "New session created: {0}",
session.getId());
session.setAttribute(KEY, new SerialBean());
        }

SerialBean bean = (SerialBean) session.getAttribute(KEY);

int serial = bean.getSerial();
bean.setSerial(serial + 1);

        // Now store bean in the session
session.setAttribute(KEY, bean);
System.out.println("***serial: " + serial);
resp.getWriter().print(serial);
    }
}
```

The main purpose of this servlet is to put a counter into the web session, and each time a user sends a request, the counter will increase by 1. Please note I've added a line of code in the preceeding class:

```
System.out.println("***serial: " + serial);
```

So we can see the output from the server console later. Now we can deploy this project into our cluster, and then we can access the servlet to use the counter. We can see the server output to determine which node is actually serving this request. Then we shutdown the working node and access the cluster again. We should expect another EAP6 server to serve the request. If the sessions are replicated successfully, we should see the counter is not reset, and it goes on increasing. In conclusion, this is an example that demonstrates the session replication among EAP6 servers.

To do the testing, we could use the cluster we've set in the previous chapters, using either JK or mod_cluster as the load balancer, and then deploy the project clusterbench-ee6.ear into the EAP6 domain.

After the preceding preparations are done and both the load balancer and EAP6 servers are running, let's access the cluster by **cURL** for the first time:

```
$ curl -cmysession.txt http://172.16.123.1/clusterbench/session
0
```

We see that the counter value is set to 0. The -cmysession.txt option tells cURL to store the session cookie in a file named mysession.txt. We will check this file later. Now we can check the server side. From the EAP6 server console output, you can see the master is serving the user request:

```
[Server:master-server] 20:10:57,810 INFO
  [org.jboss.test.clusterbench.common.session.
  CommonHttpSessionServlet] (ajp-/10.0.1.13:8259-1) New session
  created: 5LQpRPxdSCupM5eHYd93S2wR
[Server:master-server] 20:10:57,813 INFO  [stdout] (ajp-
  /10.0.1.13:8259-1) ***serial: 0
```

In the preceding console output of the master server, we can see a new session was created for the counter, and the session ID is 5LQpRPxdSCupM5eHYd93S2wR. In addition, we see the counter is initialized to 0, which matches the result from the client side.

Now let's go back to client side and check mysession.txt. Here are the contents of the file:

```
$ cat mysession.txt
# Netscape HTTP Cookie File
# http://curl.haxx.se/rfc/cookie_spec.html
# This file was generated by libcurl! Edit at your own risk.
172.16.123.1    FALSE  /clusterbench FALSE  0      JSESSIONID
5LQpRPxdSCupM5eHYd93S2wR
```

We can see that the JSESSIONID is stored in cookies. Now let's use this cookie file to access the cluster again:

```
$ curl -bmysession.txt http://172.16.123.1/clusterbench/session
1
```

The -b option will let cURL read an existing cookie file and send the cookies to the server, which means the previous session is continued. Because the counter increments by 1, it means our session is held by JSESSIONID. We can check the output of the EAP6 server again:

```
[Server:master-server] 20:26:12,496 INFO  [stdout] (ajp-
  /10.0.1.13:8259-1) ***serial: 1
```

So the counter on the master is not reset, and it keeps increasing in one session. Now let's shutdown the master server:

```
20:31:04,851 INFO  [org.jboss.as.process] (Shutdown thread)
  JBAS012015: All processes finished; exiting
```

Then we access the cluster again:

```
$ curl -bmysession.txt http://172.16.123.1/clusterbench/session
2
```

Because the master server is down, this time it's the slave server serving the request:

```
[Server:slave-server] 21:07:46,266 INFO  [stdout] (ajp-
    /10.0.1.40:8259-2) ***serial: 2
```

Though the request was redirected to the slave server, the session is held, and the counter increased from 1 to 2. This verified that the session replication works properly between two servers.

CDI-session-scoped bean replication

The usage of a CDI-session-scoped bean is similar to a web session bean. In the demo project, it provides a CdiServlet for testing:

```java
@WebServlet(name = "CdiServlet", urlPatterns = {"/cdi"})
public class CdiServlet extends HttpServlet {

@Inject
privateSessionScopedCdiSerialBean bean;

@Override
protected void doGet(HttpServletRequestreq,
HttpServletResponseresp)
throws ServletException, IOException {
resp.setContentType("text/plain");

int serial = bean.getSerial();
bean.setSerial(serial + 1);

System.out.println("***bean: " + serial);

resp.getWriter().print(serial);
    }
}
```

This servlet is also a counter, and it uses a session scoped CDI bean named `SessionScopedCdiSerialBean`. Here is the definition of this bean:

```
@SessionScoped
public class SessionScopedCdiSerialBean extends SerialBean
    implements Serializable
```

The bean is declared as `SessionScoped`, so it will be replicated across the cluster. The `SerialBean` is a POJO that holds the counter. Now we can test it in our cluster. First we need to access the servlet:

```
$ curl -cmysession.txt http://172.16.123.1/clusterbench/cdi
0
```

And then we need to check which EAP server is serving the user request. In my environment, the master server is serving the request:

```
[Server:master-server] 21:28:58,440 INFO  [stdout] (ajp-
    /10.0.1.13:8259-4) ***bean: 0
```

In `mysession.txt`, we can see the JESSIONID is stored:

```
172.16.123.1     FALSE  /clusterbench FALSE  0       JSESSIONID
+3EWwwlqUniCic9mtm6c18w2
```

Now I disconnect the master server by shutting it down, and access the cluster with the session cookie again:

```
$ curl -bmysession.txt  http://172.16.123.1/clusterbench/cdi
1
```

Now we can see that the slave server is serving the request:

```
[Server:slave-server] 21:29:58,032 INFO   [stdout] (ajp-
    /10.0.1.13:8259-1) ***bean: 1
```

As shown in the preceding code snippet, we can see that the session was replicated from master to slave.

Configuring sticky sessions with JK

In the previous sections, we have looked at how to configure and use session replication in EAP6. In this section, let's move to the load balancer side and see how we can configure a sticky session. With sticky session enabled, the load balancer will use one worker node to serve all the requests from one user. Let's start from the JK configuration. The sticky session is automatically enabled with JK. We can check this in its management console as shown in the following screenshot:

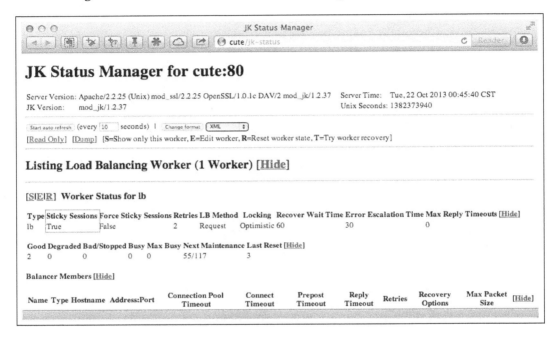

From the preceding diagram, we can see the **Sticky Sessions** option is enabled by default. Now we need to consider how a load balancer implements session stickiness: if there are thousands of user requests coming to a cluster, and if sticky session is enabled, then the requests of each user is stuck to a specific worker node. So the load balancer needs some way to record this relationship.

Storing the relationship in the load balancer is not a good idea. The relationships data will increase linearly by the number of users. The situation becomes worse if there are multiple load balancers, and then the stickiness relationship has to be replicated across the load balancers. The load balancer cannot afford to maintain this huge data and its performance will be throttled by querying the stickiness relationship.

To solve this problem, both `JK` and `mod_clusteruse` offer a simpler solution: it will put a server ID called `jvmRoute` in the JSESSIONID. The `jvmRoute` value is UUID, so it can be used to identify each worker node. As the `jvmRoute` becomes part of the session ID, the load balancer will directly extract it from the JSESSIONID and knows which server this session is bound to.

To enable sticky session, we need to edit the configuration of EAP6 to set this server ID. What we should do is open `domain.xml` and add an `instance-id` element in the web subsystem:

```
<subsystem xmlns="urn:jboss:domain:web:1.4" ... instance-
  id="${jboss.server.name}">
...
</subsystem>
```

The element `instance-id` is the value of `jvmRoute`. We've used `${jboss.server.name}` to be its value. This is a variable provided by EAP6, its value is the server name set in `host.xml`. So we know the value of `instance-id` for our two EAP6 servers are `master-server` and `slave-server`.

To reflect the configuration in EAP6, we need to put these two names into `worker.properties` in the httpd side, so that JK will know the name of its workers. Here are the complete contents of `worker.properties`:

```
worker.list=lb,jk-status

worker.master-server.type=ajp13
worker.master-server.host=10.0.1.13
worker.master-server.port=8259

worker.slave-server.type=ajp13
worker.slave-server.host=10.0.1.19
worker.slave-server.port=8259

worker.lb.type=lb
worker.lb.balance_workers=master-server,slave-server
worker.lb.sticky_session=1

worker.jk-status.type=status
```

 We must ensure that the worker name corresponds to the `instance-id` settings in the domain controller, so JK can find the correct servers that the session sticks to.

Now we can test our cluster with the `clusterbench` project deployed in the previous sections. We can still use the cURL command to access the cluster:

```
curl -cmysession.txt http://172.16.123.1/clusterbench/session
```

From `mysession.txt`, the JSESSIONID is:

```
JSESSIONID      8az1BX6Q+TQI+P4wids6BPMV.master-server
```

We can see the session is divided into two parts separated by a dot now. The first part is still the session ID and the second part is the `jvmRoute` carried in session, and its value is `master-server`. In the server output, you can also notice that the session has been created and the session ID displayed on `stdout`:

```
[Server:master-server] 22:34:42,700 INFO
  [org.jboss.test.clusterbench.common.session.
  CommonHttpSessionServlet] (ajp-/10.0.1.13:8259-1) New session
  created: 8az1BX6Q+TQI+P4wids6BPMV.master-server
[Server:master-server] 22:34:42,701 INFO  [stdout] (ajp-
  /10.0.1.13:8259-1) ***serial: 0
```

With the information in `jvmRoute`, load balancer will stick the following requests from the user to `master-server`.

Configuring sticky sessions with mod_cluster

To enable sticky sessions in `mod_cluster`, we need to add some configuration in the `mod_cluster` subsystem of EAP6. For the standalone mode, we can configure the `*-ha.xml` profiles that contain the `mod_cluster` subsystem; for the domain mode, we can edit `domain.xml` of the domain controller.

The sticky session is enabled by default by the `mod_cluster` subsystem. Meanwhile, `mod_cluster` uses the same scheme like JK to handle session stickiness, so we should also add the `instance-id` configuration in the web subsystem:

```
<subsystem xmlns="urn:jboss:domain:web:1.4" ... instance-id="${jboss.
server.name}">

...

</subsystem>
```

That's all we need to configure. We don't need to do any configuration on the httpd side, because `mod_cluster` will discover the worker node dynamically. Now we can start our cluster and check the management console of `mod_cluster`:

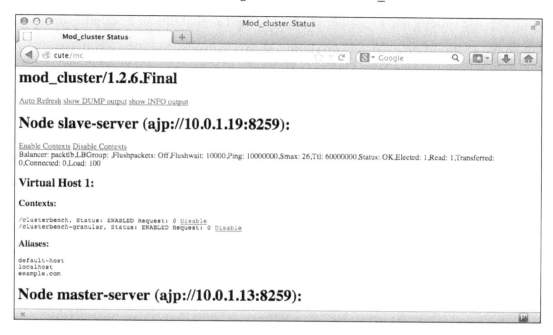

From the previous screenshot, we can see two EAP6 server names become `master-server` and `slave-server`, which means the setting of `instance-id` is enabled. Now we access our cluster:

```
curl -cmysession.txt http://172.16.123.1/clusterbench/session
```

And then we check the contents of `mysession.txt`:

```
JSESSIONID          AcJIPZwHmlauwxi82s45VWWw.master-server
```

We can see the JSESSIONID carries the `jvmRoute` information now. So httpd will send the following requests from the user to the master server.

Summary

In this chapter, we discussed two solutions that handle the stateful applications in clusters. One is sticky sessions and the other is session replication. These two solutions are usually used together to provide high availability in a Stateful cluster.

When we are building a cluster, we should always consider building a stateless one at first because a stateless cluster is very easy to scale, and it doesn't have performance bottleneck on session replication.

Index

Thank you for buying
JBoss EAP6 High Availability

About Packt Publishing

Packt, pronounced 'packed', published its first book "*Mastering phpMyAdmin for Effective MySQL Management*" in April 2004 and subsequently continued to specialize in publishing highly focused books on specific technologies and solutions.

Our books and publications share the experiences of your fellow IT professionals in adapting and customizing today's systems, applications, and frameworks. Our solution based books give you the knowledge and power to customize the software and technologies you're using to get the job done. Packt books are more specific and less general than the IT books you have seen in the past. Our unique business model allows us to bring you more focused information, giving you more of what you need to know, and less of what you don't.

Packt is a modern, yet unique publishing company, which focuses on producing quality, cutting-edge books for communities of developers, administrators, and newbies alike. For more information, please visit our website: www.packtpub.com.

About Packt Open Source

In 2010, Packt launched two new brands, Packt Open Source and Packt Enterprise, in order to continue its focus on specialization. This book is part of the Packt Open Source brand, home to books published on software built around Open Source licences, and offering information to anybody from advanced developers to budding web designers. The Open Source brand also runs Packt's Open Source Royalty Scheme, by which Packt gives a royalty to each Open Source project about whose software a book is sold.

Writing for Packt

We welcome all inquiries from people who are interested in authoring. Book proposals should be sent to author@packtpub.com. If your book idea is still at an early stage and you would like to discuss it first before writing a formal book proposal, contact us; one of our commissioning editors will get in touch with you.

We're not just looking for published authors; if you have strong technical skills but no writing experience, our experienced editors can help you develop a writing career, or simply get some additional reward for your expertise.

JBoss ESB Beginner's Guide

ISBN: 978-1-84951-658-7   Paperback: 320 pages

A comprehensive, practical guide to developing service-based applications using the Open Source JBoss Enterprise Service Bus

1. Develop your own service-based applications, from simple deployments through to complex legacy integrations

2. Learn how services can communicate with each other and the benefits to be gained from loose coupling

3. Contains clear, practical instructions for service development, highlighted through the use of numerous working examples

JBoss Weld CDI for Java Platform

ISBN: 978-1-78216-018-2   Paperback: 122 pages

Learn CDI concepts and develop modern web applications using JBoss Web

1. Learn about dependency injection with CDI

2. Install JBoss Weld in your favorite container

3. Develop your own extension to CDI

4. Decouple code with CDI events

Please check **www.PacktPub.com** for information on our titles

JBoss Portal Server Development

ISBN: 978-1-84719-410-7   Paperback: 276 pages

Create dynamic, feature-rich, and robust enterprise portal applications

1. Complete guide with examples for building enterprise portal applications using the free, open-source standards-based JBoss portal server

2. Quickly build portal applications such as B2B web sites or corporate intranets

3. Practical approach to understanding concepts such as personalization, Single Sign-on, integration with web technologies, and content management

JBoss AS 7 Configuration, Deployment, and Administration

ISBN: 978-1-84951-678-5   Paperback: 380 pages

Build a fully-functional, efficient application server using JBoss AS

1. Covers all JBoss AS 7 administration topics in a concise, practical, and understandable manner, along with detailed explanations and lots of screenshots

2. Uncover the advanced features of JBoss AS, including high availability and clustering, integration with other frameworks, and creating complex AS domain configurations

4. Discover the new features of JBoss AS 7, which has made quite a departure from previous versions

www.ingramcontent.com/pod-product-compliance
Lightning Source LLC
Chambersburg PA
CBHW060141060326
40690CB00018B/3933